CEREBRAL PALSY
A STORY

ILANA ESTELLE

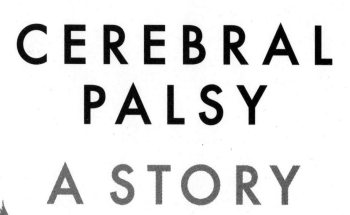

CEREBRAL PALSY

A STORY

Finding the Calm
After the Storm

Published by RedDoor

www.reddoorpress.co.uk

978-1-913062-11-8

A CIP catalogue record for this book is available from the British Library

Cover design: Emily Courdelle
Typesetting: Megan Sheer

Printed and bound in Denmark by Nørhaven

This book is dedicated to those trying to find their voice in a world where they have to speak louder, just so they can be heard

CONTENTS

Foreword   ix

Introduction: My Story   1

Chapter 1:   Understanding Cerebral Palsy   13

Chapter 2:   Cerebral Palsy, Socialising and Society   33

Chapter 3:   Family Life   73

Chapter 4:   Physical Health   111

Chapter 5:   Mental Health   133

Chapter 6:   Lifestyle, Beliefs and Spirituality   191

Acknowledgements   239

About the Author   240

Resources   241

FOREWORD

I was first introduced to Ilana and her website 'The CP Diary' in my capacity as Director of Mentor and Youth Programs at UCP WORK Inc. United Cerebral Palsy (UCP) is one of the largest health non-profits in the US today, whose mission is to advance the independence, productivity and full citizenship of people with disabilities through an affiliate network. UCP educates, advocates and provides support services to ensure a life without limits for people with a spectrum of disabilities.

Ilana has provided a longstanding service to so many through her blog; it serves as inspiration and illumination most anyone could relate to, regardless of the challenges they face ... and, let's face it, we ALL face challenges. It's hard to imagine anyone who takes the time to peruse this blog not benefitting at some level.

Ilana has given many people a community to belong to and a guarantee that their voice will be heard through her consistency with her blog over all these years. Congratulations on this amazing accomplishment.

Our lives will be forever challenging, but thankfully, there are people like Ilana who are there to offer empathy and understanding to help lighten the load a bit.

MARTY KINROSE, Former Director of Mentor and Youth Programs at UCP Work Inc.

INTRODUCTION

MY STORY

What is it like living with cerebral palsy? I cannot truly answer that question, as for forty-six years of my life I never knew that's what I had. It was only in March 2009 that I was finally diagnosed with cerebral palsy.

I was born the second of premature twins. How did I feel as a child, growing up? Those times were enormously difficult for me. I was an angry child living in the depths of despair. Some days I felt isolated, angry and misunderstood. Other days I felt frustrated and alone.

I was out of touch with reality because I had no idea what I was dealing with. I was also out of touch with my thoughts, primarily because I had no understanding around my physical, mental and emotional issues. We didn't talk about my disability: my issues were never brought up unless I talked about them, then they were dismissed as if the condition didn't exist. But it did.

I know there was a diagnosis of cerebral palsy at the age of two, because I now have a letter in my possession for a referral to a specialist as there were concerns about my balance. When my twin was beginning to crawl, I would fall, try to get up, then fall again. It was never something I could control, but how I wished I could. My mum noticed I was falling, instead of crawling. My dad, on the other hand, was not unduly concerned, and said everything would be OK.

Growing up, I felt different for all the wrong reasons. I knew there were things I struggled with. I didn't like being angry, although every now and again my kind side would appear, and I would somehow be able to separate the two issues. There was Ilana with the condition, and there was the 'real me'.

A few years later I remember telling myself that I was glad to be me. To this day I don't know why I said it; I just knew I wasn't always unhappy being me. I also knew that deep down I wasn't a bad child. I was a child with a disability I knew nothing about, and emotional issues that weren't being addressed or going away.

Although I spent a lot of my formative years being angry, it would take forty-nine years for my father to say that I was the most kind, caring and considerate of his children. In order to earn his acceptance on a disability I didn't know I had, I found myself conforming more than any of my siblings.

In fairness to my mum, she tried to deal with me but couldn't cope. She was always singling me out to do my exercises, at a time when my siblings were doing something they wanted to do. I became irritated with this, and nine times out of ten I would fight the system and become angry at the injustice of it all.

My mum would tell me I couldn't have a pretty face without a pretty leg. I never made the correlation because I didn't know what was wrong and because nothing was ever explained to me.

In my yearly consultations, questions were never asked about my condition and how the condition presented, mentally, emotionally or physically, which I began to think a little odd. With my notes now in front of me, I know the original diagnosis of spastic monoparesis at the age of two and a half wasn't correct, because I have two limbs affected not one, and my leg isn't spastic. This diagnosis was unknown to me at the time, and for most of my adult life.

Since my diagnosis at the age of forty-six, I have had to work everything out for myself, to bring my symptoms and the right diagnosis together. I have little muscle tone from the hip to the ankle on my left side. I also have a 'foot drop' and my leg on my left side is three-quarters of an inch shorter than my right side. This explains why, as a child, I would drag my leg and walk toe-heel all the time. The specialist never raised the fact that because of my 'foot drop' (a paralysis or muscular weakness which makes it difficult to lift the front part of the toes and foot) I would experience bunion issues. Years later I had a bunion removed.

Going out for walks my father would often walk behind me, telling me to stop dragging my leg and pick my foot up; I suspect he knew that was impossible for me to do. As time went by, and as a consequence of him picking me up on those things, I struggled with walking in and out of rooms, for fear of people watching me.

I hated looking at myself in the mirror and hated having to do exercises even more. When I was standing straight, I was lopsided because I had a leg length difference. When I spoke to my mum about it, she would reaffirm, 'I couldn't have a pretty face without a pretty leg.' With hindsight, without her realising, she confirmed she was aware of my diagnosis.

When I wore skirts, the lack of muscle tone in my left leg was visible, so people stared. I would limp and trip up when I got tired. I hated that. I also hated that I walked toe-heel, that I dragged my leg and I couldn't pick my foot up. I hated even more that I was being picked on for something I couldn't change and that was becoming an issue. I hated that I struggled to fit into shoes and that when I did manage to get shoes to fit, they wore differently. I was also upset at having to wear a heel lift underneath my shoe to compensate for my leg length difference, and that eventually I had to have shoes made for me that made my foot look even more deformed.

I also struggled with my handwriting. I hated not being able to write properly, or spontaneously, made worse if I had to write in front of someone. For example, writing a cheque at a till was difficult, writing anything in fact. I continue to struggle to write and with the way I form my letters.

Since my cerebral palsy diagnosis, my neurologist has explained that the part of the brain that controls my motor skills functions is also affected, so that explains the problem with my handwriting.

As a consequence of my parents wanting me to be the same as my siblings, my issues lay dormant for many years, as I continued to physically, mentally and emotionally struggle.

4

I lacked and craved mental and emotional support. It didn't help that I was born in the 1960s, a decade in which disability was commonly brushed under the carpet.

For fifteen years of my life I went to physiotherapy once a week, the Athletic Institute for exercises in May once a year, and the hospital in February once a year. All those visits seemed to eat into my childhood. As a result of my struggles, I lived a somewhat insular life, hiding a lot of my issues behind a timid façade.

But not knowing what my condition was always gave me a quiet confidence that tomorrow was another day and that things would change, and I would get better. To this day, I believe it was precisely because I had no idea of what I was dealing with: that gave me hope.

At the age of twenty-five, just before my marriage, my father wanted me to see another specialist. It felt like I was being signed off. At this consultation, the new specialist told my father about scoliosis for the first time. It was yet another condition I didn't know I had as a little girl. He also made it clear I would always have to exercise. I never made the connections with everything that was said in the consultation, because I failed to realise until I was in my mid-forties, after finding out about cerebral palsy, that I also had scoliosis.

I was told by my neuro specialist that I was perhaps lucky, because back in the day, with a disability like mine, I would have been considered a spastic and would have had to attend a special needs school. He was clear about that. He said I would have had to wear callipers, so having my issues ignored was probably a better option.

In that same consultation, I was referred to a neuro physiotherapist who did more strength tests, who told me that my arm was also affected. So, not only was I dealing with a bad leg and a 'foot drop' but I was also dealing with cerebral palsy in my arm. That would explain the weakness from my elbow to my hand, on my left side.

Knowing what the condition is now, I know my foot, leg and arm will never magically right themselves. I now have to deal with cerebral palsy in the knowledge that this is not something I can ever sort out. In my head yes, physically no.

Finally, with a diagnosis and what I now know about cerebral palsy with the help of my neurologist, I have been able to bring some closure on what I've written here. Continually having to fight my corner to be heard and listened to; feeling out of my depth mentally and emotionally; being out of touch with and wanting things to be different: all emanated from not knowing what was wrong with me.

I had to find a way to cope with anxiety, with my bad thoughts, with myself and with my life; also to try to find a place with my family alongside my difficulties and hoping that one day I would wake up and this would all be a bad dream. I just didn't get what was so difficult about telling me and helping me.

Learning more about my father over the years, I now understand why he couldn't deal with me or my disability. His insecurities were deep, he struggled mentally and emotionally to cope, everything had to be perfect; my disability was something he couldn't deal with.

What took the greatest emotional toll on me was coping with the difficulties around the disability itself, on my own, with a lack of others' understanding. It would take me until my mid-thirties to make the correlation between my anger and the reason for it.

Not having had the support I so desperately needed so that I could at least function 'in my own normal' meant that I retreated into my own little world: it was a world that I was familiar with and one that understood me. I was extremely happy there. There I didn't have to think about things. Subconsciously I had already worked out that things would never change, and *I* would have to. But even through those times, I wasn't giving up. I wasn't done yet.

It is true to say that I failed at most things. In games lessons at school, I managed easier sports such as netball and rounders. Opting out of certain games lessons, like high jump, wasn't an option for me, even with a sick note. Where I needed understanding, there was none. I had no choice but to conform.

I was expected to be the same as my siblings: no allowances were made. My brother and sisters seemed indifferent to my struggles. Perhaps, like me, they also didn't understand. If they did, they didn't say. That can't have been easy for them.

Because my diagnosis and my symptoms were kept from me and everyone else, through an institution that could have helped me, my education was always destined to fail. Where my teachers could have asked questions, they didn't. My schools were aware that I was falling behind my peers academically, because concerns were being expressed by teachers at parents' evenings, but no one ever acted on those conversations and I was left to struggle even more.

I have my own view on why my schools didn't say anything. A contributing factor was receiving no support from home, in the same way my specialists had no cooperation. I have a letter that was written by my specialist to a colleague, expressing his concerns for the lack of cooperation from my home over my mental health. The letter he got back raised concerns and stated that without parental cooperation, there was nothing he could do.

Eventually, at the age of sixteen and with few exams behind me, I had little choice and was enrolled on a secretarial and shorthand course at college. I fell into line with the idea, but I wasn't happy about doing the course.

Having struggled throughout my school years feeling like I'd failed, I went to college and continued to struggle. Although I continually felt embarrassed about my education and couldn't get past that, I am not seeing that as my issue now.

In college, it didn't help that I was given a manual typewriter that I struggled with, because of a weakness with my left hand that I didn't know was weak. There were only a handful of electric typewriters available at the time, and I wasn't chosen to have one. I remember struggling to press the keys down on my weak side, and despite having told my typing tutor, she still told me to continue with the manual typewriter. I also remember being told to speed up in typewriting speed tests, but still I continued to fall behind. It was confusing because I didn't know why I couldn't do any better.

That was one issue. Another issue, as I've already mentioned, was that I had a hard time getting shoes to fit because of my bunion and 'foot drop', so in the first year of college it was arranged that I would have my bunion removed in term time. Having been absent from college for around five weeks, I had an enormous amount of catching up to do. The operation wasn't a success, and a few weeks later I headed back to hospital, for a second operation.

On my return I continued to struggle. I felt embarrassed that others were making progress and I wasn't. My being put through college seemed like a 'box-ticking' exercise.

After leaving college, I moved into the working world and although that didn't start off too well, things slowly improved once I'd moved to a leading firm of lawyers in the city centre. It was a large and prestigious company and I soon settled into working life. Within a year I had moved my way up to working for a partner in commercial property law. I excelled and began making a name for myself.

After a couple of years and more late evenings than I cared for, I requested a move to another department and went to work for a new partner who had just joined the firm, this time in commercial litigation. It felt good that I was making strides again. I had made friends and was happy for the first time. That company was my working home for the next few years.

But even though I was making excellent progress in my working life, my education was still an issue for me. I was working with people who had done well in school and who had been more successful than I had, and their academic success made me feel even more inadequate. Emotionally,

I was still struggling with the feeling that I had failed. I couldn't move on and continued to carry the guilt, because no one had owned up to being responsible.

I had already thrown my school reports away because I couldn't bear to read the comments. I honestly felt that I should have been able to do better. Then at the age of forty-four I went back to study, but this time I chose a course in something I had an interest in. I was mentally and emotionally ready to have a go.

I opted for distance learning because it was something I felt I could tackle, and it worked. I had tutors to help me if I needed them, but I had already learned to listen to my intuition and felt I could study on my own. I couldn't study full time because my concentration was poor, so I studied a little each day. I was making headway for the first time. It felt good.

I have now gone on to complete a few accredited diploma courses from two different colleges and passed each course with distinction. I have put my success down to a culmination of using my intuition, not putting myself under too much pressure and working at my own pace. I easily completed each course, within the required two years.

I had grown in confidence and had begun to understand my life a little more; now I felt it was the right time to do something to change other parts of my past. I knew I couldn't move on emotionally without it. I consider that finding out about my disability and starting 'The CP Diary' are both part of my personal success.

My 'Diary' has allowed me to put my experiences into context for the first time, for me to understand what those are. From my initial cerebral palsy diagnosis at the age of forty-six, it would take another ten years to find out about autism, my additional disability: and to realise that I am more mentally and emotionally disabled than I am physically.

Having got married and had my first child, I went into temporary work for about a year, then decided to leave to set up my own secretarial business. I did that for a couple of years and was enormously successful at it, then I continued to work from home before having my second child.

Nothing in my life was ever going to be different unless I changed, and that's pretty much how things worked out. No one else was going to change, I had to take control. I could have simply continued to fall into line, but instead I chose to make a fresh start. I was still struggling with not knowing about my disability. I needed to find out what it was, and about myself. That was important to me.

Now with a diagnosis behind me and for the first time wanting to do something positive. I started looking into the possibility of setting up a website. Months later 'The CP Diary' was born: it became a blog that allowed me to work through my life with cerebral palsy, and to offer advice based on my experiences. Finding out about the 'real me' has been a unique and life-changing experience that has forced me to stand back and look at my life anew. It fundamentally changed the way I feel about what happened to me, and about myself.

I see that going back into study, finding out I had cerebral palsy and autism, and starting 'The CP Diary' are all instrumental in how far I have come. When I started 'The CP Diary' I literally had no idea what I was going to write about. But my website enables me to make sense of all my experiences: it has become a platform, for me to share my thoughts and to use my expertise to help myself and others, also.

There is very little information out there for those of us dealing with cerebral palsy, but I will never stop looking, or reading and writing about it, and putting what I know into my blogs. I live with cerebral palsy, but I choose not to be defined by it.

My website gives me a platform to write about my feelings, put information out there and hopefully get some feedback from others, who share similar experiences. Even if their experiences differ from mine or they don't have cerebral palsy, I still believe we can help and support one another through my blog.

It is only when our resources are pulled together that we can change the way we feel about what we deal with and eventually how we perceive others. I believe education and support are both very important tools.

Would I change my life? Would I have wanted to have come into my life if I had known what lay ahead? Knowing what I have achieved personally and with 'The CP Diary', I think my answer would have to be 'yes'.

CHAPTER 1

UNDERSTANDING CEREBRAL PALSY

Cerebral palsy is more commonly abbreviated to 'CP'. It can occur if a baby's brain doesn't develop normally in the womb or is damaged during or soon after birth. 'CP' is a blanket term commonly described by loss or impairment of motor function, but unless you have or know someone who has CP, it isn't always easy to understand exactly what it is. Because different parts of the brain are uniquely affected, the nature and extent of symptoms will vary from one person to another.

My 'Understanding cerebral palsy' blogs on my online 'The CP Diary' website shed light on my own symptoms and, for those of us living with the condition, incorporates blogs on our emotions.

AN OPPORTUNITY

It would take my mum's terminal illness for her to open up, to give me a small detail about my birth. I was in my mid-forties when she told me that my birth had been a difficult one. It must have been something I subconsciously held on to, because when she passed I decided to find out what had been wrong with me for all these years. After an initial visit to my GP's surgery, a consultation and an MRI scan, cerebral palsy was finally confirmed. For the first time, I was able to start piecing together some of my cerebral palsy symptoms.

It is usual for any new mums in the UK to give birth through the National Health Service: the NHS is hugely experienced and well equipped. However, I now know that in my case – a multiple birth and having been delivered by a consultant – cerebral palsy could have been prevented if I had been delivered by a midwife instead.

I find it incomprehensible that society seems to be complacent about the fact that so many babies are born with the condition, rather than trying to find ways to reduce that number.

In 2009, when I initially found out I had cerebral palsy, my neurologist explained that the incidence of babies born with the condition was the same as when I was born, in 1963. I find that staggering. We cannot afford to be complacent about cerebral palsy.

MY NEW CEREBRAL PALSY DIAGNOSIS

At the age of two and a half I was being treated for a spastic monoparesis, although I didn't know I had been diagnosed. Then, at the age of forty-six, after I had arranged an MRI scan, I was diagnosed with the same condition.

When I was referred on to a neuro physio, she noted that two of my limbs were affected, not one, which made my diagnosis spastic 'hemiparesis', not 'monoparesis'.

At the time of diagnosis at forty-six, I must have unconsciously been inquisitive about the first diagnosis, because I found myself looking at the notes from my last consultation with a new specialist, who collaborated with his team to assess the scan results. His letter clearly states 'the birth-injury problem'.

It is hard to believe that not only was I unaware of the original diagnosis, but it was also incorrectly diagnosed. Had I known about my diagnosis as a child, I would have been living with the wrong diagnosis thinking it was right and would never have stopped to question it.

My initial diagnosis and MRI was in 2009 and my last consultation one year later, in 2010. The correct diagnosis is 'mild hemiparesis cerebral palsy'.

The original diagnosis never made any sense to me because I have an abnormal variation in muscle tone on my left side, not spastic or floppy limbs. Years on, and now finding out about my diagnosis as a child, it makes no sense. I had no working muscle mass on my left side and yet I was diagnosed as having 'spastic cerebral palsy'.

SECONDARY EFFECTS OF CEREBRAL PALSY

Being born with cerebral palsy meant that I would always have to deal with a wide-ranging variety of secondary conditions as part of the condition. These very much depend on the extent of the impairment and which part of the brain is damaged. I deal with some, but not all, of these conditions.

Secondary examples are outlined below:

→ Deformed bones and joints

→ Sleeping issues

→ Bladder and bowel control problems

→ ADHD or ADD

→ Issues with digestion

→ Low bone density

→ Seizures and epilepsy

→ Heightened or reduced sensitivity of smell, sound and touch

→ Respiratory issues

→ Difficulty feeding and swallowing

→ Poor nutrition absorption

All secondary conditions resulting from the initial damage can change as we age, and that can make what we deal with harder. It is the secondary conditions that interfere with our ability to cope with our disability.

'My advice to other disabled people would be, concentrate on things your disability doesn't prevent you doing well, and don't regret the things it interferes with. Don't be disabled in spirit as well as physically.'

STEPHEN HAWKING

MY SPINA BIFIDA DIAGNOSIS

Although I initially dismissed having spina bifida because I had no obvious symptoms, my medical notes clearly state that at the age of fourteen in 1977, that is what I had.

In that same consultation, and again in my notes, the specialist confirmed that I would have some 'mental retardation', the extent of which he wished to assess through my development. In today's society 'mental retardation' is classified as 'learning difficulties'.

A cerebral palsy diagnosis is never straightforward and is specific to the individual. The neurological symptoms linked to each case change how a person will function, and the symptoms they have that are linked to the original presenting condition are not always evident, as my circumstances have shown.

Having looked through my notes once again, in the same consultation with the specialist on the 'mental retardation' diagnosis, my father's opinion was that my inability to learn was due to a 'poor memory' and that is what the specialist repeated back in his letter to my GP.

What I find difficult to get my head around, is that where my mental and emotional needs should have been met, they weren't. I find that difficult to comprehend. My mental and emotional challenges were ignored. Where my symptoms were dismissed and I was told there was nothing wrong, it intensified my resolve.

Not knowing about my diagnoses and symptoms as a child means that I am now having to learn about and work through them as an adult. As I continue to write and uncover more of my symptoms, I am linking everything together so I have a fuller picture of my disability.

I am thankful I have my online diary to help me piece my disability and experiences together.

NEW UNDERSTANDINGS

Following my initial cerebral palsy diagnosis at the age of forty-six, I am still putting pieces of the jigsaw together. Thankfully, I now have a better understanding of my diagnosis.

I have mild cerebral palsy hemiparesis (left side) caused by a bleed on the brain before I was born. That ties in with my mum's understanding of my birth being difficult. Mild cerebral palsy hemiparesis is a weakness in one side of the body. It inhibits growth and development, impairing the muscle and nerves controlling movement that presents as mechanical symptoms, and results in difficulty with walking, balance and motor control, little to no strength in the arm and leg, and leg length difference.

I have learned that as a result of cerebral palsy I also have comorbidity, which is the presence of one or more disorders co-occurring with a primary disorder, that in my case forms part of the cerebral palsy diagnosis.

My psychological, neurological and emotional difficulties are as a result of additional brain impairments, arising through comorbidity, in the form of Autism Spectrum Disorder (ASD), although it is difficult to know how much of that is ASD-related.

NOT KNOWING GAVE ME HOPE

It is hard to imagine how not knowing about a diagnosis can give you hope, but for me, that is just what it did. I lived with hope, hope in the belief that I would get better and that whatever was wrong with me would right itself. I was comforted by hope.

I believed that what I was dealing with was only temporary and that with each passing day, through exercise, I would physically heal. Looking back, those thoughts, although conflicting at times, saved me.

But doing my daily foot exercises and seeing no change in my foot shape, meant I must have subconsciously known that my foot wasn't going to heal, but I go back to hope: I saw my other issues as challenges to be met, and that made me believe I would heal. Of course, today I think and know differently. My foot isn't going to heal and neither is my leg. I need to be realistic.

Looking back, through my spiritual beliefs, I believe the spirit of the universe was trying to protect me, because even though no one else was asking or answering my questions, I wasn't quite prepared to give up on myself. I wasn't done yet. Although I never understood what was wrong, I continued to live with the hope that I would find out more, or at least get a diagnosis. I never gave up on that. As a child, those thoughts continued to remain and be my primary focus.

If I had given up, I wouldn't have learned about my diagnosis, or my symptoms, and I certainly wouldn't be writing my memoir. It's easy to throw in the towel, but whatever our circumstances, I still believe it is important we continue to live with hope.

We must want to evolve, to learn, to grow, to change. It doesn't alter how we get to where we are, or what our experiences are, they will always remain the same, but through growth, we allow ourselves to move on into a much better headspace. I believe we owe it to ourselves to live with hope and to strive for the best possible outcomes.

DEALING WITH CEREBRAL PALSY ISSUES

I have always equated the problems with my handwriting to my father walking behind me as a child. Now my neurologist has confirmed scar tissue is the reason I have problems with my handwriting, rather than the emotional scarring of being watched as a child.

Although others have no idea of my daily struggles, just filling in a form is difficult. Because handwriting is something we learn as a child, I feel embarrassed that I continue to struggle with it. I hope that my blog shows others that we all have struggles that we face and that it's OK.

Even now, however, I don't know how much of my handwriting issue is down to scarring, or how much is down to my father watching me walk. That is something I'll never know. All I do know is that I have difficulty with my handwriting.

MY CEREBRAL PALSY JOURNEY

Having looked through my medical history again, I now have a fuller picture of my cerebral palsy. My neurological consultant confirms that my MRI scan shows: *'An old stroke in the distribution of the right anterior cerebral artery and there is extensive damage to the right frontal lobe and a part of the right parietal lobe.'*

These two lobes are part of the four that make up the cerebral cortex. As these different hemispheres are interlinked, it would be easy for most of those lobes to be affected, either directly or indirectly. Working through my symptoms, this is certainly what has happened to me. The brain is organised in three inter-connecting layers that work together and include the central core, the limbic system and the cerebral cortex. Areas within these oversee all forms of conscious experience, including emotion, perception, thought, movement, balance, arousal, as well as many unconscious, cognitive and emotional processes. I am aware that because of my unique brain damage I struggle with each of these everyday functions and in my case, these areas of the cerebral cortex aren't receiving signals from the central core.

Each lobe has a different but related function. The frontal lobe deals with motor control and movement, the parietal lobe deals with the main sensory receptor for the sense of touch and spatial interpretation, and the temporal lobe deals with auditory perception, language comprehension and visual recognition.

> 'The best fighter is never angry.'
>
> LAO TZU

A LETTER TO MY CEREBRAL PALSY

When we deal with a physical problem, it's important we learn to embrace and accept our physical limitations, so that we're OK with them. As a form of acceptance, I thought I would write a letter to my cerebral palsy. This is how it went.

Thank you, Cerebral Palsy, for keeping me grounded, allowing me to understand and learn values of courage, compassion and perseverance through having to deal with you. Having you with me has shown me a different and better way to be. You have given me a much deeper understanding and meaning to many of my physical experiences.

I don't consider you as a disability, neither do I consider myself disabled. Cerebral Palsy doesn't define me, instead I have chosen to adapt. I cannot live my life with you, without adapting to living with you. I have learned over the years to work alongside you and will always stick up for you when I need to. The day I was born, you and I became victims of circumstance. It's not something we asked for, but something we got.

I think it's important others understand you and how your symptoms manifest themselves in me and what I have to deal with. Although the two go together, there needs to be more understanding for us, from other people. Unfortunately, there is a lot of ignorance around you and therefore the ignorance is around me too, which makes my life difficult and which others don't always seem to appreciate.

As we continue to journey through life together, I choose to embrace my life with you. I know that from a stroke at birth, we were saddled together. Thank you for teaching me how to physically and emotionally live one day at a time.

Although it took time for me to make the connections with you and to know what you were, I always knew deep down we were somehow closely connected and now that I know, I think it's OK.'

CEREBRAL PALSY STATISTICS

Recent figures suggest that the annual number of babies born with cerebral palsy, which has been relatively steady for the last fifty years or so, may be falling.

In developed countries, the rate of cerebral palsy is about 2 to 2.5 per 1000 live births. The United Cerebral Palsy Foundation estimates that nearly 800 000 children and adults in the United States are living with the condition, and about 10 000 babies are born with it each year. The condition is significantly more common among infants born weighing less than 3.3lb (1.5kg).

A study carried out at Liverpool University in the UK (by Dr Mary Jane Platt, *The Lancet,* January 2007) looked at changes in cerebral palsy rates recorded at sixteen European cerebral palsy centres from 1980 to 1996. The study found that the rate of cerebral palsy in very low birth-weight infants and those born at less than 32 weeks dropped from 6 per cent of live births in 1980 to 4 per cent in 1996, despite an increase in the number of very low birth-weight babies. The study noted that this decline was caused by a drop in the incidence of the most severe type of cerebral palsy and was probably due to improved care at and around the time of birth.

Commenting on the Liverpool University study, Case Western Reserve University in Cleveland, Ohio, said the findings were consistent with their research on low birth-weight infants, adding that despite the encouraging decrease in the prevalence of cerebral palsy, there is no cause for complacency as the condition is still associated with major disabilities.

Other research teams in the UK, Denmark and Sweden have also found evidence that the cerebral palsy rate among low birth-weight infants has begun to fall, but other studies from centres in Australia and Emory University in Atlanta (Sarah Winter MD, et al., *Pediatrics*, December 2002), have not shown a fall.

The study carried out in Atlanta from 1975 to 1991 found a modest increase from 1.7 to 2 per 1000 babies who survived for at least a year. Of most concern is that this trend was primarily attributable to a slight increase in cerebral palsy in infants of normal birth weight, although no change was seen in low birth-weight and very low birth-weight infants.

After investigating possible links to foetal heart-rate monitoring and caesarean deliveries, Dr Steven L. Clark MD of the University of Utah (*American Journal of Obstetrics and Gynecology*, March 2003) concludes, 'Except in rare instances, cerebral palsy is a developmental event that is unpreventable given our current state of technology.' (Source: https://www.psychcentral.com)

More could have been done to prevent my problem, had my mum not had to wait so long between my twin's birth and mine. Being born one hour later than my twin meant there was a high likelihood that both my mum and I would get into difficulty. The length of time between the birth of the first and second twin should be within fifteen minutes and no more than thirty minutes. (Source: https://www.ncbi.nim.nih.gov)

Although in the 1960s, when I was born, technology wasn't as advanced as it is today, human error is a significant factor. My case has proved the risks could have been minimised.

It is not enough that we put cerebral palsy down to a birth problem. There are cases of premature birth and of things going wrong at the time of birth, or in the womb. The prevalence of cerebral palsy births in the UK is about two per 1000 live births. (Source: https://www.nice.org.uk))

HOW A CEREBRAL PALSY BRAIN WORKS

A close friend of mine gave me this thought, which I want to share. Think about how difficult it is to run backwards. This is how it feels for people with cerebral palsy to move forwards. The more we try and concentrate, the slower our brains work.

I never understood why, if I do too much, my brain will periodically switch off. The physical signs associated with cerebral palsy are clear, but to the untrained eye, we appear to think in the same way as everyone else.

However, what we deal with is very different. We are cross-wired mentally and emotionally. My neurologist has confirmed in several discussions that my brain has rewired itself to compensate for the injury, and as a consequence it is cross-wired.

Because of a lack of research on adult cerebral palsy, there isn't a lot of information out there: and although that makes it frustrating for others who have to work around our limitations, it is always harder for us.

THE EMOTIONAL STRESS OF LIVING WITH CEREBRAL PALSY

Generally, I am a positive person and deal with my problems with fortitude and positivity, but when I am around people who are negative, I too feel negative: then I have to build myself back up again.

It is only through talking about mental health that we will be able to make the link between emotions and health. Our emotions play a big part in whether we will stay well or not. Emotional health can affect our immune system, so keeping ourselves in a good emotional state is very important.

People like me living with cerebral palsy don't only have our conditions to deal with, but also other people's inability to understand our problems. This can cause extra emotional stress and it's that which knocks our immunity.

UNRAVELLING MY SYMPTOMS

One size doesn't fit all when it comes to brain damage and cerebral palsy. Each part of the brain that is damaged is unique to the individual, and that is the main reason why there is limited research on the condition.

It is impossible to ascertain the exact symptoms each individual will have to face, and the medical profession's brain scans are only able to provide a general analysis of the likely effects arising from damage to a specific part of the brain.

Unravelling my own symptoms, I know that I have extensive damage to the frontal lobe, which includes the pre-frontal cortex. This controls planning, problem-solving, selective attention, behaviour and emotions. Because my emotions are impaired I get to deal with a certain level of immaturity. I also have impairments in attention span and organisational ability, and I struggle with motivation. The damage to this part of my brain is the reason why I also missed out on my milestones as a child.

I have problems with the rear part of the frontal lobe which controls motor function. Both the left and right parietal lobes contain the primary sensory cortex that controls sensation, such as touch. Where someone with cerebral palsy can be undersensitive, I am oversensitive. An associated area controls assessment of textures, size, weight and shape. I have damage to the right parietal lobe. The damage here also means I have spatial awareness difficulties, resulting in not seeing and bumping into things, difficulty naming objects, trouble finding words when I'm talking, and some difficulty with both reading and writing. I am slow to read and have difficulty forming outlines when I write.

I struggle to navigate my way through recognition and am unable to feel certain emotions that other people take for granted. It is my intuition that helps me manage my daily routines.

But piecing my symptoms together isn't a problem for me. In a way I welcome it, because it allows me to evaluate my life where I didn't have that before. Understanding why I am as I am is long overdue. What I mind is being judged for my shortcomings, with a lack of tolerance, empathy and understanding from others.

CEREBRAL PALSY AND LIFESTYLE

As a child, and not knowing I had cerebral palsy, I continued to hope that by completing my exercises, my physical disabilities would disappear and that whatever I had would right itself if I just persevered long enough.

How wrong I was. In general terms, treatment for cerebral palsy focuses on ways in which we can maintain and improve our quality of life, our lifestyle and overall health. I was always aware that I needed to look at my lifestyle, and being born premature meant that would inevitably become an even bigger priority.

A baby who is born full term and who has cerebral palsy may not face the added complications of a baby who is premature and who is born with the condition. But it is important for everyone living with cerebral palsy to look at their lifestyle, so they may improve their quality of life.

Even though I was considered 'normal', my life was far from normal. Living with cerebral palsy means my central nervous system is affected and although I don't have difficulties with eating or swallowing, I do have digestive problems, reflux and irritable bowel syndrome (IBS), made worse because of cerebral palsy, and because I was born prematurely. Those difficulties continually interfere with my lifestyle.

It is scary not knowing how I will age with the condition and what further complications I will encounter, as my brain cells deteriorate. Another reason why it's even more important I concentrate on living a healthy lifestyle.

A healthy lifestyle is important for everyone, but particularly for those of us who have cerebral palsy, because it is a condition that brings additional complications.

> 'Try not to associate bodily defect with mental, my good friend, except for a solid reason.'
>
> CHARLES DICKENS, *DAVID COPPERFIELD*

THE TIES THAT BIND

Blogging on my website 'The CP Diary' has allowed me to document my experiences with cerebral palsy, after finding out that is what I'd been struggling with up to the age of forty-six, when I received my diagnosis.

I also talk about the fact that it wasn't a freak of nature that caused me to have cerebral palsy, but a mistake by the consultant and nursing staff, leaving my mother for too long in the delivery room.

The course my life has taken would never have been any different. If you believe things happen for a reason, my writing is the reason. The process where you grieve for the loss of something you don't have, as a consequence of something that has happened to you, is what I feel I am doing.

I was born with physical, neurological and emotional issues. Never being able to share my thoughts growing up is another loss. There are questions I may never get the answers to. The only answers I will have, are those I answer for myself in my head.

FINDING CLOSURE AGAIN

Having already seen one neurologist when I was first diagnosed with cerebral palsy, two years later I opted to see another neurologist, so I could try to find out a little more about my symptoms, and, although the consultation wasn't altogether a success, I came away with more positive thoughts.

I went in with no preconceived ideas, hoping that my neurologist could shed some light on more of my symptoms. I wanted to be given another chance to work through my symptoms, so that I could link my experiences with more of my presenting symptoms.

Unfortunately, I forgot that he would already have notes from my doctor in front of him. Although that made it slightly more difficult, I came out knowing a little more than when I walked in. I gained a clearer understanding of which part of my brain is damaged, and which parts of my body this accords with.

My neurologist went on to explain why my leg is worse than my arm and explained in more detail which part of the brain was responsible for that.

It is not possible to be certain which of my daily symptoms are attributable to my cerebral palsy, my neurological issues, or which symptoms are due to my having been born prematurely, but my neurologist thought that cognitive behavioural therapy (CBT) would help with brain fatigue. Having started CBT, I have found that it has helped with my anxiety, and it has indeed also helped me to cope with my brain fatigue.

Ever since I was first diagnosed with cerebral palsy, I have worked tirelessly to find out as much as I can about it. The more I meet with a brick wall, the stronger my resolve. Ever since I can remember I have always worked with logic. If something makes sense and I understand it, I go with it. The problem I have is that I know what I deal with is logical to me, but because there is little or no information out there, it's not always easy to verify my view of things.

I knew that when I started my journey, I wasn't guaranteed a diagnosis, let alone an understanding of my symptoms. However, in many ways, knowing a little more about both has made life even more frustrating for me. When we have no information at all, we tend to muddle through without asking questions and accept where we are.

Speaking my own truth for the first time brings a little comfort. Getting my thoughts out there for others to listen, helps.

CHAPTER 2

CEREBRAL PALSY, SOCIALISING AND SOCIETY

My 'Cerebral palsy, socialising and society' blogs incorporate the everyday challenges of living with a disability I didn't know I had, whilst coping with different aspects of emotional stress. Despite all of this, I still believe we can build a better life for ourselves, alongside what we have to deal with, and still have social time.

Although I have CP, it's important that I and others in the same position also find ways to handle everyday stress. Unconsciously, I have always known that having a disability would bring about more stress for me and that has turned out to be true. Stress-busting and finding ways to deal with stress is the difference between good or ill health, and us being social. The more we challenge ourselves to cope with and work through stress, the more engaged we will be.

ATTITUDES AND DISABILITY

Although I was never considered a child with special needs, I was a special needs' child, just like any other child with a disability. Whether we're a child or an adult, when it comes to a disability, we're somehow expected to fall into line, and our struggles can sometimes be met with resentment from those close to us.

The reality for some of us is that where others should be emotionally supporting us, we often have to be our own emotional support. Attitude is important for those of us who deal with a disability: and attitude starts at home with our parents and family.

If society is going to permanently change attitudes towards disability, it is initially up to parents to instil inclusivity and kindness in their children.

My suggestions for disability inclusiveness are as follows:

→ Don't see anyone with a disability as a problem, or someone that needs to be fixed;

→ Not all people with disabilities present in the same way, so it's important to understand each disability separately and how each person presents;

→ Compassion, patience and kindness are important. They go a long way towards communicating and understanding what someone with a disability deals with.

Those of us who have a mild disability may struggle even more than those with an obvious disability, because our shortcomings aren't always apparent to others, and we're still expected to conform. Being around someone who deals with a disability can teach us about ourselves, but we must be prepared to look for the understanding.

If attitudes changed towards disability and people were generally more positive towards those with one, there would be less of a stigma towards disability, and disabled people would fit into their lives more comfortably.

What has happened to empathy, tolerance and understanding? Because that is all it would take. If the shoe were on the other foot, others would expect nothing less from us.

COMPASSION AROUND DISABILITY

I find it difficult to watch documentaries that talk about disabilities, not because I'm afraid to watch, but because I feel bad for those who were also born with a disability. I know what they feel, because I feel it too.

I think more of us need to be tolerant around those of us who have a disability. We're the same: we may present slightly differently, walk and talk differently, but we feel pain – physical and emotional – in the same way everyone else does. That makes us the same.

It is important for everyone with a disability to feel comfortable with themselves and around other people, therefore what others say and how they say it matters. Not everyone will know how to act around disabled people. They may often find it difficult to make eye contact with them. They may not always know what to say, or how to say it. It is also important for someone without a disability to know what someone with a disability needs. For example, always ask before giving assistance, not all people with a disability want or need it. Also, avoid showing pity or being patronising.

People genuinely aren't always comfortable with disability, there can sometimes be a slight awkwardness. I believe that's because disability isn't talked about like it should be. When I was growing up disability wasn't discussed, and the subject was considered taboo.

Yes, society is doing slightly better, but people with a disability are still considered broken. Disability needs to be understood; understanding is something that needs to be encouraged, so that everyone knows how to behave and interact around someone with a disability.

Society still isn't great at inclusion, but disability has always been here. It needs to be inclusive. Disability is now being championed more by people, including members of the British Royal Family, but for inclusion to work fully and across the board, disability needs to be considered and seen as normal.

CEREBRAL PALSY PARENTING

A study by Newcastle University reported in *The Journal* in October 2014 (http://www.thejournal.co.uk) suggests that children with cerebral palsy tend not to suffer a diminished quality of life; I think it all depends on our parents and family, because this is where the emotional support starts.

It is important for any child with a disability to have the input and support in the same way other children do. In some circumstances they may need more. All children need to be connected with parents, siblings and friends for their own psychological wellbeing.

It is not easy being a parent of a child with a physical disability. Although it can sometimes be difficult for parents to understand how to look after a child with a disability, they must continue to handle them appropriately.

It is when parents have a lack of understanding of their own needs that they will have a lack of understanding of their children's needs. As a result, their children may struggle to develop a sense of individuality.

But a lack of awareness must not be an excuse for a lack of understanding. It is also not a reason to hold a child back. When children grow up with a disability they should always be encouraged to engage emotionally with their siblings and friends.

When we have a sense of self, we are more likely to develop confidence. We are no different from able-bodied children in that respect, we just have different needs.

We must all learn about people's disabilities so that we can be more informed about their needs. Sadly, those with a disability are sometimes invisible: they are usually spoken at, rather than spoken with.

For those who have a disability, standard procedures may get in the way of personal conversation and contact, but everyone with a disability must be, and deserves to be, engaged directly.

If that were to happen, their relationship with those who support them would be a lot richer and more rewarding.

MY SCHOOL LIFE

I hated school because I struggled, both socially and academically. OK, let me rephrase that, I liked school, but school didn't like me. I found it difficult and isolating. I had no understanding of why I struggled, I just knew I did.

Why I struggled to learn would only become apparent to me years later: I struggled because of neurological difficulties and rewiring from cerebral palsy. I never stood out, I merely existed; or perhaps I did stand out, because it was obvious I was different.

I was slow to learn and struggled academically and with my handwriting. As I said earlier, I still have my handwriting to deal with. It's not like a broken leg where everyone can see the problem and can sympathise. Handwriting is something we learn at an early age. I'm embarrassed that it is something I struggle with, but to keep it a secret would make me feel worse.

I hope that writing this book will show others that we all have something we struggle with, therefore we shouldn't feel embarrassed, or bad about it. Others need to understand what we deal with.

When it came to school, falling behind was a daily occurrence and being told to speed up on my handwriting was another. When the rest of the class had already got their notes down from the board, I was lagging behind.

Looking back, I find it odd that my teachers never asked why I was struggling. In school I was slow to understand even the basics of what I was being taught. To take the stress and anxiety away, I emotionally withdrew. My school reports highlighted issues, all of which were ignored. There was also no follow-through between home, school, and parents' evenings, or the grades on my reports.

Although my parents could see that I struggled, and mum had her concerns, my father always said I would catch up. In the meantime, I was continually being picked on in school, for a lack of substance in my homework and schoolwork. I didn't know my lack of ability had anything to do with my neurological impairments and cerebral palsy, because I didn't know about either, but I did begin to sense as much.

There was no joined-up thinking. I was well-behaved in school, but mentally I had already given up. Growing up, I was considered lazy. If anyone thought I was stupid, they didn't say it to my face. The irony is that this wasn't a lazy issue: I was struggling mentally and academically through a disability I didn't know I had, and with no support, I continued to struggle even more. Years later, my successful studies and website show a different story.

With the right support and guidance from home and school I know I could have achieved a little more. Although it would take me many years to work out how to learn and be successful, I have now found a different way to learn that works for me.

BEHIND THE MASK

I sometimes think that living with cerebral palsy is like living behind a mask. Only someone with cerebral palsy will understand what that means.

It is difficult for me to work through each day, without feeling as though everything is a chore. I find it difficult to be present in long conversations and will periodically find myself switching off, or have difficulty connecting and hearing in the first place. That frustrates me even more.

Because there is a lack of understanding of what I deal with, it's easy for others to comment. I try to remain upbeat, focused and positive more times than I'm not, but that proves difficult and I still feel I'm on my own most of the time.

It is very hard for me to motivate myself, and the older I get, the more challenging it becomes. Emotionally, I find it hard to switch off from the psychological problems associated with the condition.

There are days when I have to force myself to refocus again, so that I can psychologically move forward from all the negativity surrounding my condition, but I know I will have to go back to the same thoughts, until I feel emotionally stronger.

It's a challenge being challenged. Cerebral palsy tires me out and it's a constant chore.

AUTISM SPECTRUM DISORDER

Since my cerebral palsy diagnosis at the age of forty-six, it has taken me an additional ten years of research to understand my presenting neurological symptoms and to find out those were part of the autism spectrum. The answers I have from my diagnoses explain who I am, how I am, and how I've been. They also explain my experiences to date. Those all fall into place now.

Every question, every uncertainty, every mental struggle has now been ticked and crossed through autism, that I didn't know I had as a child. Autism is a co-occurring condition of cerebral palsy. Even before a confirmed diagnosis, after coming into contact with someone with symptoms similar to mine, I knew I was dealing with the disorder.

Although autism and Asperger syndrome were historically seen as two different conditions, today Asperger's is no longer a separate diagnosis. It is now a part of Autism Spectrum Disorder (ASD). In 2013, *The Diagnostic and Statistical Manual of Mental Disorders* (DSM-5) changed its classification.

Over the years, I have acquired knowledge of my experiences through my heightened senses, focusing on the things I needed to focus on, to bring me the answers I needed, to the exclusion of everything else. ASD also explains my struggles with touch, loud noises, textures and smells.

I see things with greater clarity through my heightened senses, experiencing the world in a very visually focused way. I work with my intuition, which cannot always be explained by thought or fact, but rather through a deep inner feeling, without having to find or look for it.

Having ASD is the reason I think and write in the way that I do. I know that without my website I would never have been able to work my symptoms out, in any great detail. It has become my lifeline to a better existence, enabling me to uncover the reasons behind my experiences.

ANXIETY AND AUTISM

There is no getting away from the fact that as a child and through my school years, I lived with anxiety. As an adult I still continue to live with anxiety. I also now know that my anxiety is linked to ASD.

There are many common behaviours seen in those with autism that overlap with symptoms in other anxiety disorders, therefore familiarity and understanding for someone with autism is very important.

Where autism creates fear, panic and anxiety, with the help of a CBT counsellor, it has become easier for me to talk about the issues that cause me anxiety.

Anxiety disorders affect 42 per cent of autistic children compared with just 3 per cent of children without autism. Mental-health issues affect 79 per cent of autistic adults, but many of those adults won't get the help and support they need. Two in five autistic people are diagnosed with an anxiety disorder, but many more will go on to experience symptoms of anxiety that affect how they live their lives. (Source: https//www.autistica.org.uk)

With autism, we may struggle to work through situations, not because we don't want to, or because we don't trust other people's judgment, but because autism makes it difficult for us to understand conversations and the meanings of those conversations. For us to be comfortable with our choices and for us to feel settled, we must have understanding.

Not having the first will cause a ripple effect on the second. New circumstances, any changes to our routine, and new environments will cause us to feel anxious.

MY AUTISM MODEL

Post-autism diagnosis, and I'm still working through it, trying to get to grips with my symptoms. Below is the autism model that my consultant says is relevant to me.

Some of the information is taken from the letter from my neurologist, explaining my particular brain damage, which I gave to my autism specialist. The following is an extract from my autism consultant's letter. He goes on to explain in more detail my strengths and difficulties that have identified me as being on the autism spectrum.

UNUSUAL SENSORY EXPERIENCES

More than nine out of ten people with autism are thought to experience their senses differently to those without autism. These differences usually affect more than one of the senses and include over and/or under sensitivities to hearing, smell, touch, taste and sight.

If too much information is presented, it can overload the senses. This describes a disorder of brain function which affects emotion, learning ability, self-control and memory, and which unfolds as the individual grows.

NEURODEVELOPMENTAL MODEL OF AUTISM

The brain damage in the right frontal lobe at birth has made me becoming autistic more likely, brought about through cerebral palsy.

This model of autism is relevant [to me] as it outlines that the parietal and temporal lobes part of the brain (that is affected) may process much more information than a person without autism, but processing too much information can lead to delayed sensory processing such as being slow to find objects in a cluttered environment.

In contrast, with people with autism, the ability of the frontal lobe to function when stressed is often impaired, leading to problems with short-term memory, switching tasks, reorganising oneself in response to sudden changes and understanding others.

It typically modulates emotion and attention, preventing emotions getting too high or too low, so that they're more balanced. This can lead to a pattern of 'hyper-focusing' on a particular interest, or difficulties when it comes to concentrating on mundane tasks.

It is sad to know that some of my struggles didn't have to be struggles, but I am also grateful that finally I have managed to bring answers to symptoms I never knew I officially had.

MY EXPERIENCES WITH AUTISM

I grew up only knowing about a bad leg and foot, so having an autism diagnosis is the biggest thing that's happened to me. With an autism diagnosis, I now have understanding. It is the reason why I struggled, why I would continually start something and give up, and why over the years I was labelled as being lazy. It is the reason I didn't understand school and the reason why I couldn't learn.

It also explains why, when I was asked why I wasn't doing my homework, my standard answer was, 'I don't know what I'm doing.' Giving a name to my symptoms for the first time allows me to stand back and exonerate myself from any blame, shame, guilt or supposed wrongdoing.

The consultation in January 2019 confirming I have ASD is now somewhat of a blur. For now, my autism diagnosis seems to have reinforced the whole disability thing and how I got to this place. I feel it has come too late in the day for me to be told something I should have been told as a child. It also feels good, however, that I have never chosen to define myself by either condition.

Yes, I have mild cerebral palsy and I have autism, but if I can use what I know about both conditions to understand myself, and for others to understand me, I will have really achieved something.

OTHERS UNDERSTANDING AUTISM

Autism must be explored by others so that they may understand how we present. Those of us with autism can get a bad press because others don't understand us and because they can find us intense.

I have spent most of my life trying to adapt into a normal life with a neurological disability I didn't know I had. My life would never be normal. Thankfully times have changed and disability is more accepted today, but when it comes to disability, it is not up to us to fit in, it is up to others to make sure they're inclusive.

It is important others are mindful of what autism is and how we may interact. Because we may struggle to fit in, it makes it even more important for others to understand and want to help us.

Although autism presents differently for each of us, autism isn't difficult to understand. The more others choose to learn about what we deal with, the more they will understand us. Once they become better at understanding, they will be better equipped to help us modify the situations that cause us difficulties.

It is important for others to help us focus on what they know we can do, rather than what they know we struggle with.

MY AUTISM IS A GIFT

When I found out about my cerebral palsy, I wanted to do something positive for the first time. I'm not really sure why I thought about a website, apart from the fact that it seemed like a positive thing to do. With my diagnosis, I could start researching and writing about my disability. Recently diagnosed with autism, I must do the same, so that I can understand and come to terms with my neurological difficulties.

Finding out that I had cerebral palsy in my forties and autism in my fifties isn't how I wanted my life to play out, but I now know why my life had to happen like that. I have always known there was more to my problems than what you could physically see. It was important I found out.

Through autism, being able to see everything in black and white is a gift. It allows me to see issues and situations as they are, rather than how I would like them to be. Because of my damaged brain and heightened senses, I see things from a totally different perspective and although that is hard in terms of communication and social acceptance, I have become more accepting of myself and therefore don't always feel I need to fit in.

My writing and blogging is also a gift. I am able to do what I do because I have autism. Although I find it difficult to express my thoughts verbally and relate those back to people, I have no problem expressing my thoughts on paper and online, on my blog.

Uniquely, even as a child, it was a gift that was with me. I didn't know it then, but it is a part of me now and I love it.

FLAT AFFECT

Every time I write a personal blog and I think I'm done learning about myself, I find out something about myself that I didn't know.

I used to stare in the mirror as a child, not because I was vain and I liked looking at myself, but because my facial expressions seemed flat. I didn't know that was a thing until my cognitive behaviour therapist mentioned it to me.

The term 'flat affect' is used to describe a lack of emotional reactivity, typically observed in people with autism. It is a failure to express feelings, especially in response to issues or situations in which we would normally be expected to engage the emotions.

A person with the condition rarely shows expressive facial gestures and/or animation in facial expression, or change in voice. A person with flat affect has nearly no emotional expression, or no expression at all. When I smile, my facial expressions are fixed instead of being naturally animated. I also talk in a flat and monotone voice.

Out of necessity, and using my intuition, I have taught myself to read people's facial expressions and social cues. Through my blog, I think about my emotions and write them down, rather than show or talk about my emotions face to face.

I can't believe how much work I've had to do on myself, just to function 'in my own normal' despite my neurological difficulties, and the fact that at the age of fifty-six (at the time of writing) I am still learning about myself.

> 'You must not lose faith in humanity.
> Humanity is an ocean; if a few drops of the ocean are dirty, the ocean does not become dirty.'
>
> MAHATMA GANDHI

DEALING WITH STRESS

Stress is the feeling of being under too much mental or emotional pressure. If not dealt with, it can affect how we think, feel and behave on a conscious and subconscious level. Although we're not always aware of it, the mind and body constantly interact. If we're struggling mentally, this can have a direct physical effect.

Stress is a state of emotional or mental strain, or tension, resulting from demanding and adverse circumstances. Stress isn't tangible, we can't touch it, but it's there, and not always when we expect.

When it comes to stress, I have to think about and deal with each issue as it arises. Because I deal with autism, the more I struggle to work through an issue the bigger the issue gets; the more I mentally struggle, the more anxiety I deal with, the more panicked I feel. Taking stress away helps me deal with my emotional and physical issues with more ease. It also allows me to focus on staying positive, so that I can make better decisions, particularly around health issues.

I believe there are ways for us to deal with and limit stress. For example, saying 'no' to unreasonable demands from family, particularly if their demands are likely to create more stress. We need to think about whether what they're asking is fair. If the demand was placed on someone else, would we see it as fair?

As children, we're not always able to say no. But as an adult we are entitled to say no, particularly if we can justify that response with reasons rather than a list of excuses. We are refusing the request, not the person. A compromise must be reached: we could try offering an alternative. If the time isn't right but the request is, an explanation will help the other person understand why.

We must look at the issues and the people that are causing us stress. Rather than wait for stress to pass, we must deal with it when we experience it. Things always feel different with the benefit of hindsight.

We also need to manage the issues that are causing us unnecessary stress. Plan new and positive experiences, so that we can focus on what we have to gain. We must be honest with ourselves so that we understand what we're finding stressful, even if someone else might see it as trivial. It's not for them to judge.

WE CREATE OUR STRESS

If I were to tell you we are responsible for our own stress, you would probably laugh or shrug it off. You may even get cross; after all, who wants to be told they are the reason for their own stress?

I'm not sure how many of us are open to that idea, yet it's a fact that stress is self-generated. Others will contribute to our stress, and although we don't have control over their behaviour and the way they behave towards us, we do have control over how we deal with our own stress.

This may be seen as something negative, but it's actually quite constructive. Anything that makes us self-aware is a good thing, but we must also make ourselves aware of where our stressors are coming from, so that we can acknowledge and accept that we can do something about those. Addressing stress through our thoughts and behaviour will always help reduce it.

I stand back from myself so that I am able to see the bigger picture of the particular issue I'm dealing with. That helps me understand certain elements of the issue, like the first time I came face to face with my mum's terminal illness.

Internal stressors can include uncertainty, a particular worry, our inability to control a particular outcome, or our reaction to it, and, in certain cases, depression. Beliefs are also a factor, as are our opinions and expectations, particularly the expectations we put on ourselves.

External factors will also play their part, but it's up to us to be responsible enough to pinpoint and understand where they are coming from and why. External factors mean stress will always be present in our lives, but by being attentive and with the right attitude, we can control the amount we let in.

EMOTIONAL DISTRESS

Other people's distress may affect our emotions within moments of us being in their company. After some exposure to emotionally distressed people, we may begin to feel distressed ourselves. When we learn to recognise our stress, we will find it easier to recognise it in others. I grew up around stress, so I was aware of what some of the signs were from a very early age.

Some emotionally distressed people will remain distressed, rather than deal with their emotions: we all know that dealing with our feelings is not easy. But despite all attempts to help them, some people would rather not change. Instead, they will continue to make excuses or blame other people for their lives, making everything about others and nothing about themselves. Everything becomes personal.

They will avoid taking responsibility for themselves, even if their state of mind makes them ill (although, in their defence, they won't always know their problem is emotional distress). That said, emotionally distressed people can grow into healthier people, just by staying open-minded and accepting they may need help. It is important we all take responsibility for our emotional health and our behaviour.

Stress isn't tangible, it's not something you can see or touch, but you can learn to recognise its signs. Unfortunately, stress will impact relationships more than any of us acknowledge, or are aware. Because stress has become part of everyday life, we've almost become immune to its warning signs and symptoms. It's easier to see stress in others than it is to recognise it in ourselves.

Even when we manage and deal with our own stress, other people's stress can affect us. It's hard when others don't recognise their own stress, but think we are the catalyst of theirs. In today's society that aspect of stress is commonplace.

Stress will always show up in verbal and non-verbal communication, especially in quarrels and arguments. In some cases, when stress is left undetected, it can make you feel disconnected from others. Stress can create anger and may even cause isolation and depression in those who already have a predisposition.

It is important we learn to recognise the signs and symptoms of stress in ourselves, and equally important we don't carry other people's.

THE INNER VOICE

Our thoughts around cultural beliefs can be the catalyst for us holding on to negative emotions and struggling with anxiety. Those thoughts may tie us to a set of beliefs that don't always form part of the spiritual process.

Walking this path sadly doesn't always allow us to question why we're taking that path, or whether that path will help us on our own inner personal journey. By letting go of conditioned thoughts through our cultural beliefs, we may be able to let go of negative emotions and anxiety.

For us to take our own personal journey, we must learn to channel our inner thoughts, paying attention to what's going on in our head, so that we become aware of our inner dialogue. We must get rid of the mental clutter and learn to concentrate on ourselves, and use our emotions in ways that allow us to get to know ourselves better.

Once we get rid of the mental clutter, we can begin to concentrate on the 'whole'. We must simplify our life by removing the physical clutter, so we can have better mental health. We need to think about the invisible force that's around us and bring empathy, tolerance and patience into the equation, so they become part of us.

Feeling connected to something bigger than ourselves will give us a sense of purpose and bring a sense of meaning into our lives and with each other. When we can understand that everything around us is aligned and we know that 'things happen for a reason', we will begin to take control of that which is within our reach.

Being spiritual is a lifestyle choice that needs to be continually honed. Spirituality keeps our lives real and helps us connect with our higher selves. I listen to that 'knowing little voice' and it brings me the answers I need.

COPING MECHANISMS

As a diverse society, we develop different strategies to fit in with the wide variety of people we come into contact with. This goes back to our childhood, to our parents' parenting and to our experiences: from our parents to their parents, through the generations and through the environments they grew up in.

For example, a child who is particularly bright may be picked on because of his or her abilities in school, or the child with a disability may be picked on because he or she looks different.

The child who is picked on because he or she is particularly bright may work hard at home, but give the impression that in school, he or she is like everyone else. A child with a disability may see their disability as someone else's problem, if they feel secure. But if they are insecure, they may see themselves as the problem.

We all have different coping mechanisms. As individuals we are unique, but these situations aren't. Where some of us will work relentlessly through our challenges, others won't, and they will start to blame others. My coping mechanism was to emotionally withdraw.

I don't remember if I was bullied for being different, but I do remember feeling isolated and being stared at in and out of school, because I physically presented differently to everyone else.

Given all my difficulties, I struggled with school, homework and exams. In school, I struggled to fit in and keep up with my school work, and although I didn't give up on school, school gave up on me.

For many years I carried the guilt because I saw myself as being responsible for those failings. Now when I look back, I reconcile and know my failings had nothing to do with me. They were neither my fault, nor my responsibility.

'The saddest aspect of life right now is that science gathers knowledge faster than society gathers wisdom.'

ISAAC ASIMOV

RESENTMENT

Resentment comes from feeling we've been treated unfairly, when we find it hard to forgive those who have wronged us.

When we hold on to negative experiences we will begin to harbour feelings of resentment. The more we hold on to negative experiences, the more we close ranks on our feelings, the more those feelings of resentment will intensify.

But holding on to resentment prevents us from seeing our life in a healthy and balanced way. Resentment fuels anger that if left unchecked, can turn into abusive and self-destructive behaviour.

I was angry and irritated by the injustice of being kept in the dark, having to work through my mental, neurological and emotional issues on my own. When I am able to understand the person behind the deed, I am less inclined to judge.

When someone doesn't want to know, and they struggle emotionally, as a result they will continue to struggle. But how they are may not always be down to a malicious act or a malicious thought, it may be because that person can't cope.

It doesn't make it right, it just makes it what it is. All we need to know is they will always be accountable and responsible. It's not for us to judge.

Where resentment is concerned, we tend to push those feelings away without thinking about or dealing with them: perhaps it's because we would have to confront ourselves first before confronting others and emotionally we're not quite ready to do that.

Maybe we're also worried that saying something will jeopardise the relationship and we're not keen to rock the boat: but if that's what we're worried about, it's clear the relationship has already hit rocky waters, and if that is the case, then it's time to reassess.

DEALING WITH REPRESSION

As a child, I held back and kept my emotions to myself, partly because no one was listening and partly because my childhood wasn't a happy one. It was my coping mechanism.

When we talk about 'repression of emotions', we are talking about holding our emotions back. It's a means of survival so that we don't have to deal with uncomfortable emotions. It's a technique used temporarily to help us manage our issues, so that we can obtain emotional stability through painful situations.

Repression helps us block out unwanted thoughts, feelings and memories that if we were to think about would make us first feel irritated and upset. It involves projecting our feelings and attention away from our conscious thoughts into our subconscious, blocking out hurtful memories. Repression must only be used temporarily.

It is important we tap into our subconscious and deal with the emotions we constantly put on the back burner, so that we can tackle issues head-on. Not talking or addressing issues can seem like the easy way out, but eventually the issues we ignore will begin to make us physically and emotionally sick. There is no quick fix to emotional healing, but actually wanting to heal is a good place to start.

CRITICISM

Being self-critical stems from our core beliefs which, unless corrected, will continue. But how many of us are aware that each time we say something we're being critical, or even self-critical? Therefore, we shouldn't take offence if someone points out that is what we're doing.

In the early days negativity wasn't something I was consciously aware of, but the older I got the more I became aware of where my negativity was coming from. Childhood can sometimes be a breeding ground for negativity.

But as long as we're aware, with understanding and practice, there is no reason why we cannot change. It's all about perception: how we choose to see ourselves and our life. We must embrace new perceptions.

If someone tells us we're being negative, we should accept that we probably are. This can be the first step in recognising those traits in ourselves. What others say should always be taken as constructive and not personal.

However, some of us will use criticism as a weapon. Those who are critical don't think about the way they speak, they just speak. They'll bleat something out, then perhaps think about what they've said after they've said it, by which time it's too late to retract their words.

But critical people are critical because of how they feel about themselves. We should remember there is always a bigger picture to someone's emotions. People don't just let off steam at others because they want to hurt them. They're not always consciously aware of why they're not happy, or why they're feeling angry. Those feelings are usually buried in the subconscious.

I remember attending prize-giving for my daughter, when the head teacher talked to the pupils about 'constructive criticism'. She was trying to impress upon them that the harder they worked in school, the more they would achieve. She was referring to the students who didn't work during the academic year, stressing that if they began to work, they could do better next year.

Her point resonated. I believe there is a difference between criticism and constructive criticism, and how easy it is for us to take both personally. If the person we're talking to benefits or improves from what is being said, then constructive criticism has to be a good thing.

We need to remember that when we hand out constructive criticism, the person we're talking to has to receive it as constructive. If we fail to get that across, we're automatically setting ourselves up for failure even before we've begun.

Statements like, 'I need you to…' or 'I want you to…' won't help us. All they'll do is make the other person go on the defensive.

Any criticism works better when it's offered with the right attitude. When there is a negative history between two people, it won't make a difference: both must change their attitudes. When we take a team approach and use words like, 'Let us look at…' the other person is less likely to go on the defensive.

Constructive criticism is used in schools and colleges, by parents and other institutions where learning takes place. It may also be used to manipulate other people into believing what's being said, instead of as a tool to help.

ACCEPTING CRITICISM

As soon as someone criticises us, we feel the need to retaliate. As a child, I didn't notice because I was too angry, but criticism is nothing more than another person's observation of us: if there is an issue there we must deal with it, but first we must recognise it. The problem we have with criticism, is that what others see is not normally how we see ourselves. Instead, we think of it as a personal slur, but that's not what it is: it's a slur on our behaviour, it's our behaviour they're struggling with.

In some cases, the people who see us in that way are probably right, but because we're in denial we don't see what they see. We resent giving others the satisfaction of them knowing us, but if it's family or friends they are usually well versed, in the same way we are well versed with them.

People will often tell us things that are in our best interests because they care, but we won't always see it that way. But if we are prepared to listen, another person's viewpoint will always give us the opportunity to learn something about ourselves. When we're too quick to defend ourselves, we will fail to learn.

It is usually only when we have calmed down and we use that time to reflect, that we see they're right. Trying to see another person's point of view, or agreeing, will always defuse what could turn into a heated argument.

Accepting criticism gives both parties the opportunity to remain calm and stay friends, particularly as what's said is often given in good faith. We must learn to see it that way.

BEING SELF-CRITICAL

Being self-critical stems from our core beliefs, which, unless corrected, will continue. But how many of us are actually aware that every time we say something, we are self-critiquing? We need to be aware and not take offence when someone tells us that we're being self-critical and negative about ourselves.

When we grow up surrounded by negativity, it's not something we will always consciously be aware of, but as we grow and we begin to take more notice of our environment, we will become more aware of the family dynamics and negativity.

Being positive can sometimes be difficult if you're living around negativity, but we must make a conscious decision that where we are subjected to negativity, we aren't going to participate in being critical about ourselves.

By understanding family dynamics and our lives better, and with practice, there is no reason why we can't shift from being self-critical to self-assured. It's all about our perceptions, how we see ourselves and how we perceive our lives. But if someone tells you that you are being self-critical, you should perhaps listen.

The first step is to recognise our behaviour patterns. What others say about us should be taken as constructive and not personal.

REINFORCED INSECURITIES

Deep-rooted emotions will always affect our energy and how we feel. It is important we think about issues that are making us unhappy and deal with them. But no matter how we feel, the buck stops with us. We must be responsible for our behaviour, regardless of the self-limiting subconscious issues that are causing us to feel unhappy and angry. We're unhappy and angry when we have little control over our subconscious thoughts and our life.

I learned very early on that I needed to be proactive and take back control of my emotions. The negative issues I had to deal with reinforced my own insecurities and those centred around certain aspects of my past.

When I think about it, I go back to my emotional struggles around school particularly, because each day was a mental struggle, a battle. I would go to school filled with dread and come back home with the same dread, knowing I'd have to go back into school the next day. Not having the emotional support to help me work through that time never left me.

Any negative energy around us when we're small can have a spiral effect, reinforcing our issues even more. Although we may subconsciously hold on to thoughts from as far back as childhood, dealing with those thoughts can help us see things more clearly. When we struggle to deal with something in the present, something negative from our past can easily present itself temporarily.

Although my story is unique, dealing with our emotions isn't. It was not knowing what I was dealing with and struggling with my neurological difficulties that weighed heavily. For many years those overall thoughts became intertwined. Having no emotional support to help me function in my own 'normal' was difficult.

Whilst we are responsible for our own happiness, it is important we find a way through, so that we're not continually living with certain aspects of our past. It is important we continue to work on ourselves so that we can resolve our issues and so they're not reinforced every time we deal with or think about something.

'Many people die at twenty-five and aren't buried until they are seventy-five.'

BENJAMIN FRANKLIN

INTIMIDATION

It's not always obvious to us that the people in our lives may be intimidating and controlling. For those of us who deal with intimidation, it can be a nightmare because we unwittingly allow others to intimidate us without us realising. Irrational thinking is sometimes the reason we allow others to intimidate us. We must find ways to respond differently.

Being intimidated means we allow the other person to interfere with our emotions, how we think and feel about ourselves. Through intimidation, we feel belittled, self-conscious and inadequate. Although control is linked to intimidation, they must be understood and recognised as two separate problems.

When we are intimidated, we open ourselves up to being controlled. Someone whose emotions have been interfered with, who already has weakened defences, will unwittingly allow outside influences in. Sadly, we don't always make those conscious connections.

But we need to continue to show others that we will not be intimidated and that we are in control. We need to develop new ways of dealing with people who intimidate us so that we become more assertive. We must take back control from those who make decisions for us and stop the intimidation.

CHASING PERFECTION

How many of us seek the validation of others by attempting to be perfect? We convince ourselves that other areas of our lives will be all right once we have achieved it, when in reality we should be seeking to do the opposite.

The idea of a world in which everyone and everything is perfect is nonsensical. I have seen people continue to change things because they want things better than the way they have it. We must learn to consciously appreciate what we have.

As a child, I wanted to be normal, like everyone else who didn't have a physical issue. I wanted to walk properly without a limp, I wanted to walk heel-toe. I was constantly checking the heels on my shoes, to see how they were wearing down, and would get annoyed because they looked and wore differently.

When I crayoned outside the lines, I would throw the colouring sheet in the bin and start again. The outlines on my handwriting weren't formed properly, they were inconsistent and too small, but luckily that need for perfection didn't spill over into anything else.

My being a perfectionist seemed to be centred around my anger, not so much around me. For example, I used to love colouring in and if I coloured out of the lines, I'd get cross and want to start again. I believe it has something to do with obsessive compulsive disorder (OCD), which can co-exist through a diagnosis like cerebral palsy, but for those who are chasing perfection all the time it can be exhausting.

It is an impossible quest, one that will end with disappointment every time, because no one can expect to be the best all the time. The bar will always be raised. Perfection isn't something that will always be within our grasp.

But having to chase perfection can also be a stressful burden. Having to keep up standards is stressful enough, but if you must, being the best at *something* is better than being the best at *everything*. Being the best at everything means you'll never settle for second and you'll be too stressed to enjoy it.

ACCEPTING YOUR IMPERFECTIONS

Our desire for perfection and our need for inner peace will always be in conflict if we refuse to acknowledge our imperfections. However, focusing on our imperfections will take us further away from attaining inner peace. Despite our best intentions, we cannot do or give of our best when we're attached to, and focused on, the wrong things.

When we fall into the habit of wanting to change things in the pursuit of an illusionary perfection, then we must tell ourselves things are fine as they are. We need to remind ourselves of the good in our lives, and that it's OK not to be perfect, or to achieve perfection.

As we begin to eliminate the need to be perfect, we will finally make peace with ourselves. When we can make peace with ourselves and with our imperfections, we will have inner peace.

ILLNESS AND ANGER

It's easy to become angry around negative experiences, but it's also important we deal with those experiences so that anger doesn't control or consume us. Talking about how we feel can make a difference between acceptance and non-acceptance of our issues and illness.

When it comes to people with a terminal illness, it's easy to see why those people might feel angry, but perhaps their anger isn't just about their terminal illness? Anger can be an underlying trait that makes up who we are, because we have issues that are buried deep in our past.

The thought of being terminally ill can bring about a negative and angry response, but it can also bring about positive feelings, particularly in the early stages of the illness. When my mum was diagnosed with lung cancer there was a determination for her to remain upbeat. She had a sense of commitment to fight and remain positive.

Although it's the patient that initially has to deal with his or her illness, their family also need to be able to cope and work through it. When a loved one is angry all the time, it makes it hard for their family to cope. Nobody wants to be around angry people.

Unfortunately, anger stops a person from finding a level of calm and acceptance. Achieving that can make a difference to both our emotional and physical recovery. When it comes to any terminal illness, it's a lot more difficult to bring our thoughts together positively, but by standing back, we can begin to assess our illness more fully and that allows us to take more positive steps, moving forward.

If you have someone you can confide in, or you feel comfortable talking to, that will always help.

LEGACIES FROM CHILDHOOD

During a conversation with my father, he acknowledged mistakes, which helps me, but he couldn't remember all of them in any detail.

I cannot change those mistakes, but they did become part of my life and legacy for a while. The mistakes our parents make over the years do become part of our lives, but that doesn't mean we can't move on from them.

We can break childhood legacies, the mistakes made by our parents and communities, by changing our attitude, by altering the way we think about things. A lot of our life consists of repeated negative patterns that have been passed on. Those patterns are what need to change.

It is important we think about our life, write down some of what we remember, the memories that we know we have been affected by, so that we can see those patterns. At the end of the process, we can begin to understand and then start to change our own negative patterns.

NEGATIVE SELF-TALK

When I was little, I would negative self-talk so much that I worried the negative thoughts I carried would become a reality. My negative thoughts were always there, they seemed to follow me like a shadow.

What I didn't understand was that when we grow up surrounded by negativity, negative self-talk becomes our daily dialogue. I remember before going on holiday, not being able to sleep for weeks, because I was continually worried the plane was going to crash. I went on holiday and the plane didn't crash.

Sadly, negative self-talk can lead to anxiety and depression, so it is important we find ways to talk ourselves out of what we tell ourselves. We become fearful because we worry we have no control over those things.

It is when we're stressed and going through difficult times that we hone in on negative self-talk. But negativity will always feed into our psyche and that won't change until *we* learn how to change.

CHANGING NEGATIVE SELF-TALK

To change negative self-talk we must be aware of our inner self-talk and the words we speak to other people. We must always think on a conscious level about how we speak, and how we let certain situations affect us.

Unfortunately, what we think creates how we feel, how we feel determines how we act, and how we act, creates our experiences, so it's important we get those right.

Below are my pointers on how to change negative self-talk:

> → Take control of your stress so that you're being more positive. When you think and talk positively, your self-talk will reflect your positive thoughts;

→ Keep yourself busy mentally. When you keep busy, your mind detaches from negative thoughts without you knowing you're consciously doing it;

→ Stand back so that you're looking at your thoughts from the outside in. That way you'll look at situations objectively, with a view to changing what you see;

→ Surround yourself with positive people so that their positivity becomes yours.

When you can understand your circumstances, when you can see the bigger picture, you will then begin to understand the changes you need to make.

We must accept taking responsibility for ourselves. Taking responsibility puts us back in control of our thoughts and helps us create a positive lifestyle. A positive lifestyle with positive thoughts will change negative self-talk into positive self-talk.

DEALING WITH SETBACKS

Setbacks are inevitable in life, whether you're striving for perfection, or dealing with difficult people around you, but once we get beyond our setbacks, we will spend less time being concerned about them.

To deal with setbacks it's important that we have composure, because without it, it's easy for us to panic. Having composure is usually based on self-beliefs and confidence and comes with experience.

As children, we're never far away from our emotions, and trying to keep a mentally positive attitude can be difficult. When anyone has composure, dealing with setbacks will always seem easier. There are no right or wrong ways to deal with setbacks, it's what works for the individual – but we must try not to be critical of ourselves.

It's easy to look back and question ourselves, but that's counter-productive. Nothing ever stays the same, circumstances will inevitably reach a conclusion one way or another. It's important we recognise our progress through the setbacks.

However little progress we think we've made, we've probably made more than we think. Always see progress as a contributing factor, for a more positive outcome and the start of something new.

LIVING WITH NO REGRETS

For many years I carried and lived with guilt that left me angry and stressed. Each day felt like a new battle.

Everywhere I turned, my disappointments continued to stare back at me. I couldn't get rid of the guilt that was clouding my judgment on new situations, but slowly, by giving myself time and through my inner beliefs, I began to see that my guilt had nothing to do with me. I began to understand that a lifetime of regrets had everything to do with my lack of control over decisions that had been made for me. Unfortunately, any guilt or regrets we carry, regardless of whose guilt it is, will keep us mentally stuck.

It took me years to understand the concept of and deal with the guilt issues, but when I eventually let go, it felt like a release, like a weight had been lifted. Now, with a different attitude, my outlook and life has changed.

Although it takes time, it is important that we slowly begin to work on the things we need to change. Until we do that, the mind will continue to play tricks. We can tell ourselves we're OK, but we're really not when we repeatedly play back those tapes.

Any new decisions I made after that became a stepping-stone to more change and more lessons for me to learn. As I continue to evolve and grow spiritually, I rely on my intuition to help me pave the way, so that I can live with no regrets moving forward.

CHAPTER 3

FAMILY LIFE

Family life can be defined as routine interactions and activities that relatives do together. It is family that provides the love, care, protection and security, both physical and mental, for a child. Family is supposed to fulfil the needs of the child so that the child can socialise and fit into society.

It is up to the parents to encourage their children to learn about societal norms, beliefs and core values and to continue to encourage their independence as they grow. Family should want to spend time doing things together and enjoying each other's company. This is what families should be striving for.

My 'Family life' blogs incorporate all aspects of family life and show us that through challenging times, we can come through even stronger as a family.

MY GRANDMOTHER

There is often one person in our life with whom we deeply connect, who emotionally understands us and who sees the world like we do. For me, that person was my maternal grandmother.

She was a good person with a kind heart, but like me, was often misunderstood. She was quiet and unassuming and didn't take anyone or anything for granted.

She didn't show her emotions to everyone, but when in the right company she seemed to open up. Generally, she didn't talk much about herself and I knew not to ask her questions, but she did like to talk to the people she cared about.

She was the kind of person you wanted to be around and I loved spending time in her company. She was a person you didn't want to be without.

Her apartment was peaceful. It was a place that didn't feel like a permanent challenge. It became my sanctuary. She was my grandmother.

MY CHILDHOOD STRUGGLES

I feel it is important I write about the emotional struggles I experienced as a child, as they seem completely relevant now.

I've talked about negative self-talk and how that can impact our lives. Growing up, I found it difficult to shift bad thoughts. I didn't understand why. I didn't know how to move my thinking and as many times as I tried, I failed.

Although as children we don't always understand our feelings, or how to identify with what we feel, living in a negative environment doesn't help. Growing up I carried all the hallmarks of being insecure and having depression.

A lot of what we hear, see and experience in the early years plays a part in our emotions and in our lives. Insecure children become insecure adults. Nothing changes, we just become good at masking our insecurities, so the outside world doesn't see what we feel inside.

Insecurities and fears that cannot be placed or identified in that moment are also likely to go back further. I believe everything we hear or see is stored in our subconscious, recorded as a memory, together with the feelings that went with those experiences. To reduce our struggles, it's important we think about and deal with those.

REFLECTING

Peering out of the window and seeing a neighbour going out with her daughter, for a split second my thoughts went back to my own childhood with my parents, and I found myself wondering whether my neighbour would accomplish great things with her child.

I understand why my thoughts went back there. We may sometimes stop to question whether our parents have got things right for us, and then use those comparisons to quantify where we are in life, how happy we are, or how satisfied we are with our lot. Or maybe it has something to do with our less than perfect childhood.

We innately take our behaviour from our parents, but it's usually only when we stop to question what we know that we can begin to change what we didn't like, or what didn't work for us. It's only when we hear ourselves repeating our mother's words and we say, 'I'm turning into my mother' that we realise that is what we are doing.

Sometimes it's not a bad thing, but it's not always a good thing either. It just means we must work harder through our parenting, at finding a place with our own children so that they may write a positive history for themselves.

It's very hard to get everything right as a parent and it's something we may not accomplish, but if our children can see that we have done our best and that our best is good enough, then we will have achieved greatly.

I believe it's important for us to make a positive impact on our children. What we leave behind will stay with them long after we're gone. It will also give them a positive view on their own lives as they go out into the world.

It is important for us to try and get it right because it's right to get it right: so that when we're no longer around, their memories of us are positive ones.

CEREBRAL PALSY AND FAMILIES

The biggest challenge for someone living with cerebral palsy in a family is how that child can succeed alongside able-bodied family members.

Trying to manage any disability around family life is difficult. As a child growing up with something that didn't feel right, and later finding out it was cerebral palsy, meant my disability would become part of my family's life too. I didn't know how much that would affect us all.

A study carried out by the University of Alberta, and reported in *Developmental Medicine and Child Neurology*, 2001, compared families with adolescents with cerebral palsy to those without a disabled child. Some previous literature has suggested families of persons with disabilities experience more negative family relationships; however, the families in the study demonstrated similar scores in family function and life satisfaction. (Source: https://onlinelibrary.wiley.com)

The study's authors concluded that while navigating adolescence can be a challenge for a family, the presence of a physical disability does not mean that the experience will be more or less demanding.

However, the rollercoaster effects of dealing with something like cerebral palsy can be emotionally difficult and may leave less time to spend with their other children. It depends on how the parents manage their child's disability.

Ensuring that a child with cerebral palsy can flourish alongside able-bodied family members is a big challenge and although my parents spent some time taking me to the hospital and physiotherapy appointments, my mental and emotional needs were sadly not addressed.

As a result, emotionally, I struggled to cope and withdrew very early on. With the proper management of my condition, the impact for me could have been significantly reduced.

Whilst I had yearly examinations to make sure my legs were growing properly, health care professionals didn't get involved. At the age of fifteen I was told by my consultant there was nothing further they could do for me and was told to get on with my life. I couldn't because my mental and emotional needs were never met and I didn't have the tools to cope.

Also, there has to be some form of integration in families. Thankfully times have changed since I was born. There is more support available now and the physical and emotional needs of children are more readily addressed by their families.

FAMILY ESTRANGEMENT

Family estrangement is the loss of a previously existing family relationship, where emotional distancing is extensive; where there is little to no communication between individuals for a prolonged period.

Estrangement is one of the most painful of human experiences, primarily because there isn't always the understanding behind why families, parents, or siblings are estranged.

In my experience, estrangement isn't always based on physical detachment. Not everyone is in a position to physically leave. Mentally we may detach because of bad parenting, unsupportive behaviour, toxicity and abuse.

There are other reasons why family estrangement occurs, such as personality conflicts, difficult family dynamics, divorce and money issues. Having a child with special needs can sometimes be a contributing factor, but the impact can be lessened by parents bringing their children together so that everyone understands their unique set of circumstances.

From a parent's point of view, it is difficult to know what's best or how to deal with raising a child with a physical or mental disability without ignoring the other children, and yet however hard a parent tries, their attention will always turn to the child that struggles. It's the nature of raising a child with a disability.

To avoid estrangement happening, parents should attempt to make time for their children individually. Parents who prioritise spending equal time with their children will help to make their children feel loved and supported. It's important for children to have continual inclusion and for each child's needs to be met. Any issues and disagreements between siblings must be handled sensitively. A feeling of injustice, particularly within families, will lead to anger, resentment and estrangement.

It is also important that parents explain to their other children, in a language they will understand, why their sister or brother needs the extra help. When nothing is discussed and the parents' attention turns to the child that needs the most help, it is inevitable their other children will struggle too.

As a general rule, children are usually happy to go with something once they've had it explained to them. I am sure any child would be happy to help their brother or sister, if it means they will get the help they need.

FAMILIES TOGETHER

Knowing about a diagnosis will foster more understanding of the situation from for everyone, which will result in easier, more loving and symbiotic relationships.

I would have been happier with a diagnosis. I resented the labels and, without understanding what was different about me, being labelled even more. Those were incredibly hard times: being an inquisitive child meant I never stopped asking.

As a family, had my struggles and disability been handled differently, my siblings would have grown up with a better understanding of me. It must have been difficult for them.

People are not inherently jealous. Jealousy comes when attention is taken away. The spotlight was totally on me because of my difficulties and yet those difficulties were never discussed, or addressed. As I have said before, when any family fails to discuss what is being presented, distance will always grow between them. It is important families learn to talk about things, so that distance doesn't become an issue.

Families have to want to close the gaps and bring about understanding, but that is a big sticking point when it comes to a child who deals with a disability.

MY GUILTY FEELINGS

I believe that no matter how parents raise their children, they will never get it right 100 per cent. But what about those of us who continue to carry guilt over the actions of our parents? I carried guilt for not persevering in school when I found it extremely difficult to keep up and was constantly falling behind. I carried guilt when I was asked why I wasn't working, when in truth I was already struggling.

I carried guilt for not doing well in exams, and not making headway in the most important years of my life. My biggest guilt was ripping up school reports, because I couldn't bear to read my teachers' comments, and failing with my education yet never knowing I wasn't the one to blame.

I carried the guilt for years, but now see the guilt I carried had nothing to do with me. My guilt had always been a consequence of other people's insecurities and inability to guide, help and support me with a disability.

Over fifty years later and after extensive work on my physical, emotional and neurological issues, I am now in a better emotional place. I have had to learn how to pick up the pieces after years of negativity and trauma.

The opportunity to stop beating myself up about my life came just before my mum passed, when she told me that my birth had been a difficult one, and that made me think about my disability, and a new journey began.

OUTSIDE INFLUENCES AND PARENTING

My own experiences of being parented as a child weren't positive, but as a parent myself, I feel I have worked hard to be better.

Parenting is one of the most difficult jobs we will ever do. There are many challenges associated with being a parent. We play a big role in our children's lives: even before they go to school and in the early years we are their teachers, so it's important we get the parenting thing right.

As parents, we have the ability to influence our children in positive ways. I have talked about my own childhood, and although I am more positive in my approach to my own children, it would be easier for us to parent the way our parents parented us and their parents before them.

It's easier to settle into repeated patterns set by our parents, than it is to change them. But parenting children differently takes time, effort and understanding: time to work things through, effort to continue, and understanding where we want and need things to change.

Children must also learn how to behave in an appropriate manner and communicate well, so that they can grow into responsible and well-balanced adults. A positive approach from an early age helps them overcome any obstacles, challenges and barriers they may encounter.

Although parenting starts with us, it's a constant battle to compete with outside influences such as school, extended families and society. As soon as children start school, parents often begin to see a difference in their child's behaviour due to everyone else's input. Against outside influences, it's the parents who will have an uphill struggle.

Teachers play a pivotal role in children's lives too, so it's important they're on the same page as the parent: but ultimately a child's behaviour will lie with the parents.

When something goes awry, and others are to blame, it's the parents who become responsible.

RECOGNISING PARENTING TRAITS

Having taken time to reflect on what I see as my failings, particularly in school, I realise now those failings weren't my responsibility. There was no mental or emotional support in place around my disability, or my difficulties, but I also know I need to take control back and own those failings, since they're still mine.

If you have feelings of failure, below are some questions that can help you assess where you are:

→ Do you continually blame your parents for your life?

→ Are you happy to take control, or do your parents control you?

→ Do you find yourself doing the same things your parents did without question?

→ Are you continuing to repeat the same mistakes as your parents?

→ Are you continually living with the same bad habits, or patterns that you need to change?

→ Are you in a rut and don't know how to change things?

Without question, we repeat the patterns and habits our parents set out for us. Recognising our behaviour pattern is the key to long-term change: we must also be prepared to change the way we think and the way we react to things.

'He who asks of life nothing but the improvement of his own nature is less liable than anyone else to miss and waste life.'

HENRI FREDERIC AMIEL

PARENTING ROLES

The parenting role for a mum has always differed from that of a father, but I wanted to explore why it seems to be the mum children turn to when they're looking for someone to blame.

When I was little, Mum was always to blame. It didn't matter what we as children did, the finger was always pointed in her direction. Yes, Mum disciplined us, but I feel all of this goes deeper.

Society stereotypes parenting roles. While it is no longer considered the accepted norm, when I was growing up, psychologically and emotionally parents were expected to fit into their gender roles, with the mum having the biggest role. Different rules applied to each parent.

The mum seemed to be the one who was penalised if she disciplined, whereas the dad was the one who participated at his own discretion, then stepped back without incurring penalties to himself. In some cases, but obviously not all, a child's success is attributed to the mother also, as is the finger of guilt when something goes wrong.

When girls are small, they are encouraged to nurture, to care and be responsive. Boys are encouraged to be tough. But even if boys are encouraged to nurture, they do not find nurturing instinctive. While there remains debate that behavioural instincts are pre-programmed in male and female brains, socio-cultural factors are also accepted as important.

In some cases, yes, but this won't be the experience for all. When men become fathers, there are fewer expectations on them around disciplining their children, which means their personalities are left intact once their children are grown and have flown the nest. Some men are not encouraged to discipline children in the same way women are, but that doesn't mean that they cannot and shouldn't discipline.

Men can also be responsive, attentive and supportive. A lot of it is passed through the generations. Parenting is a generational and cultural thing. It is how we're brought up.

Some men are still happy to leave their wives or partners to discipline. Thankfully, some are happy to share the parenting role also.

STRESS IN THE HOME

Home should be a sanctuary, a place where once the door is closed, we have peace with ourselves and each other. Though it's easy to assume stress is all about work, homes can also be a catalyst for stress.

Children also have their own stresses to deal with, but they may not always be able to express themselves, or talk about how they feel. They may not always feel like they can talk to their parents or that their parents will understand what they are going through, particularly during their teenage years, and as parents, we may not always feel our children understand the pressures we're under.

It is hard being a child, but being a parent is harder still, with all the expectations and responsibilities that come with the role. Behavioural standards placed on children by society can be difficult for some parents. Not everyone is equipped mentally to take on the parenting role.

Being expected to parent well means the pressure is always there. Understanding each other's needs is often difficult. Others may sense when someone is stressed, but may not always be totally aware or understand why. Parents who are stressed may switch off to what's going on around them.

They may not always make an effort when they're stressed. They may also perceive and interpret discussions wrongly because their mind is elsewhere and they're not listening. Parents may also take their family for granted and therefore will make less of an effort. All of these things bring about added stress, but it's important parents are able to stand back and deal with their stress, think about what they say and how they say it, so as not to offend.

As parents, it's important we listen, it's important we're compassionate, tolerant, and caring. As a family, we must all work together to limit the amount of stress that's brought into the home. We must talk about things.

When it comes to my own children I have always taken an interest in their emotional wellbeing and mental health: I was aware of their struggles, their hopes, their fears, and when things bothered them. Although I was aware I needed to find the right balance, I felt it important my children knew they could also approach me.

Over the years, I have encouraged them to talk about things. Not having had any emotional support as a child, I understood even more how important it was to get that part of my parenting right.

PARENTS MAKING DIFFERENCES

Any parent will be catapulted into a world of uncertainty as soon as they know they have a child who is born with physical, mental or emotional difficulties.

Over the years, my father spent a lot more time with me, driving me to my annual hospital appointments. Mum took me to my weekly physiotherapy appointments after school, but when I wasn't going to physiotherapy, or my yearly hospital appointments, I was treated the same as my siblings.

At the time I didn't know differences were being made, but it's clear they were. I used to get mandatory sweets before every hospital visit, which my siblings never got. Although my hospital visits felt like the job was getting done, it was something I endured and something my siblings had to put up with.

Creating differences between the treatment of siblings can manifest itself in many ways, and although outsiders may not always see the difference parents make, children are always aware of them. For example, children who are born into families where culture is central to their lives, fall into this category, as I did. Where culture is practiced, and differences aren't made between children, children can be nurtured in the same way, serving as a basis for peaceful co-existence. Culture can provide support, tolerance and understanding. It can also provide trust.

When it comes to a child living with a disability, parents may feel forced to behave differently with that child. They may also choose to make allowances for that child because they feel guilty, or responsible. It is often how disability works.

Children will always deal with different things, but being treated differently in childhood will always manifest itself into negative sibling rivalry and adult behaviour.

GENERATIONS OF BEHAVIOUR

Family behaviour has a habit of repeating itself with future generations. Those behavioural patterns passed down through the generations will dictate how we communicate with other family members and how we get to live our lives.

Those behaviour patterns will determine our opinions, our beliefs and our decisions. They will also influence our own behaviour. As a result, we will unconsciously fail to change anything and will continue to emulate the same behavioural patterns unless we make a conscious effort to do things differently.

The truth is that if our parents don't deal with conflict, we can't avoid it. If our parents are pacifists, we will also be pacifists. As children, we learn to grow and evolve around the parameters set out by our parents. If our parents and family are positive role models, we should become positive role models also.

As each generation's traumas are passed down from generation to generation, those traumas will have an influence on our children and will pass on to future generations. Previous generations, whether they know it or not, will always have an influence on future generations.

I believe as parents, it is our job to teach our children how to develop valuable learning skills, instead of us unconsciously relying on what's been passed down through the generations.

UNDERSTANDING OPINIONS

Growing up, I was discouraged from having any opinions, but in today's society children are encouraged. It's right that children have their own opinions.

It is our job as parents to learn how to be more understanding of our children's opinions, as long as our children's views of what they want for themselves don't interfere with their health. In the same way, it is up to our parents to try to be more understanding of us and our opinions.

It isn't easy for any parent to discuss opinions with their children without meaning to be discouraging, as they continue to look for compromises between what they want for their children, what they want for themselves, and what their children will accept. When it comes to viewpoints, reaching a compromise where everyone is happy isn't always easy.

Until children learn how to channel their thinking, it is possible that their expressed opinions may be forthright, which can make discussions with their parents a little more difficult. Boundaries seem to have changed with each passing generation.

Respect looked and sounded different when I was growing up. When it came to parents having an opinion, children were more likely to conform to their parents' wishes.

A CHILD'S WISH

I am sure to some extent we can live with one or two small issues being ignored, but isn't a parent supposed to help us work through our issues, so that we make the transition from childhood into adulthood more easily?

It's comforting when the parental support we get helps us deal with our issues. Knowing a parent is there, even if they can't always help or won't always be around, should at least give us confidence that we can get through anything.

I have had to work without emotional support over the years, and although it has shaped me into the person I have become, it would have helped me cope with my disability.

That would have made my transition to adulthood a lot easier, particularly with what I have had to deal with. I would say it's a child's greatest wish.

THE SMALL THINGS

It's easy to look back on our parents' lives, to see how they could have changed things to make their family life more complete.

It's the children who lose out when parents choose to live their lives in ways that benefit them, but don't always benefit their children. Some children are made to fit into their parents' lives, not all parents will fit their lives into those of their children.

Children want their parents to be present and to offer emotional support, love and guidance. Showering children with gifts isn't a substitute, and doesn't show them that their parents care about them.

However we parent, I believe it is important we leave positive imprints on our children's lives. They are huge parts of our lives and as parents, we need to nurture that.

PARENTAL AND SIBLING ALIENATION

Parental and sibling alienation are more common than we think or understand: it's a topic that is important if we are to change how 'the family' works. Sadly, parental and sibling alienation is very real and has been around for years.

It involves 'the programming of a child by one parent, who attempts to denigrate, interfere and undermine the child's relationship with the other parent.' It also happens with siblings and can result in siblings becoming separated from one other.

It is common in families and relationships. Family dynamics can be such that this kind of behaviour is slowly introduced. Feuding families and mismatched couples may also emulate this type of behaviour.

It usually comes about because of one parent's inability to separate from conflict with their partner and they instead choose to focus all their attention on the needs of the child. Psychiatrist Richard Gardner developed the concept some twenty years ago, brought about through child custody disputes.

Fidler and Bala (Family Court Review 48, 2010) report both an increasing incidence and increased judicial findings of parental alienation; they also report estimates of parental alienation in 11 to 15 per cent of divorces involving children; Bernet et al. (*American Journal of family Therapy*, 2010) estimate that about 1 per cent of children and adolescents in North America experience parental alienation.

There is also a scholarly consensus that suggests this type of alienation is abusive to children, but unfortunately it isn't recognised as a form of abuse. The sad reality is that children do become embroiled in their parents' battles, and a child can replace the other parent as a target.

Sadly, this will not only have a marked effect on the targeted parent and their other siblings, but on the dynamics of the whole family. Although it is not recognised as a form of abuse, being on the receiving end, it can feel like abuse.

OUR PARENTING INFLUENCES

As parents, it is important we maintain our own morality if our children are going to have a chance of being raised in a moral way. The more moral the parent, the more moral the child will be.

Do we take time to consciously think about our moral standing? We know what we know, we do what we do, but we fail to think about how our actions will impact on others in the longer-term.

A parent who is sensitive to other people's feelings and injustices can influence early moral development in their children. It's what parents should be striving for. It is important for family members, including extended family; in fact anyone looking after our children, to have the same moral standing.

We should take the time to work things through, instead of leaving our parenting to chance, in the hope that our children will turn out OK. We must be empathetic, compassionate, patient and tolerant in our approach to problems.

The right influences will go a long way to help build the right foundations for children. It's not just down to the parents: influences must be uniform across the board. We should want to guide in a way that helps serve our children better.

A positive parenting approach will always have positive *influences* on children that will not only make us better parents, but will make us better people too.

SETTING THE STANDARDS

Parents set the standards from a very early age. One of the most important factors of a child's upbringing is what that child is continually exposed to, from childhood into adulthood. Therefore as parents, it is important we set the right standards.

Children are not only influenced by their parents, but by other family members too, including grandparents, aunts and uncles, etc. As those influences will also have an impact, it's important they also get the appropriate matching and consistent standards right.

The influences children have will affect every decision they go on to make in their adult years. It's fine so long as all their children's influences are what their parents want for their children, but may cause friction if other people's influences fall below those expectations.

Our values are what we attach importance to, and what give our life meaning. Other factors may include a child's education, external influences and culture, which all play their part. Values are the building blocks that form the basis of our decisions and how we live our lives. Our core values are the difference between right and wrong and good and bad.

Children will always have external influences, but if those influences set a higher standard than those set out by their parents, it can lead to family conflict. Outside influences can interfere with the parents' role, and result in the parent having to compete for their child. Parental values are important to every child. They form the foundations for success in later years.

When it came to my mum, although she didn't talk much about her values, she did expect us to have manners and to think about and put others first. Through my spiritual beliefs, even as a child, I innately knew what to do.

Away from my anger, I was a caring and thoughtful child. I remember my younger sister acquiring a money box and I went and got my pennies from my money box, so she would have money to put in hers.

I believe that our values and how we treat others are the catalyst for a more peaceful and harmonious life: couple that with empathy and tolerance and we become better people.

OUR PARENTS' PARENTING

As children, we have no idea about our parents' roles in our life, in any great detail. We don't think of our lives in that way. We assume they look after and care for us: we also assume they have our best interests at heart.

As children, we're also sometimes conditioned from an early age to accept a life our parents choose for us. They might parent the way they have been parented and the cycle continues.

Having children of my own has made me consider my own parenting skills. Children should be encouraged to make their own choices, with parental guidance.

I try to use encouragement and positivity as a means of communication with my children, and although I follow spiritual values that bring more clarity into my decisions and my life, I don't force my children to follow the same values.

Because they have had access to my values, I would like to think that some of the values I associate with spirituality, such as simplicity, understanding, sincerity, empathy, compassion and loyalty, are ones that my children will embrace further on in their lives.

Although there is no pressure, I hope they will bring their own understanding of what being spiritual means, in its wider context. When it comes to any form of parenting, it's not right for any parent to force their children's hand.

TOXIC PARENTING

There is a dividing line between occasional criticism and continual over-criticism, towards a child by a parent.

Most parents genuinely want to do their best to provide their children with a healthy and happy upbringing, but some parenting can be toxic and may result in future therapy sessions. Toxic behaviour, if allowed to continue, can cause emotional and mental damage to a child. Some of the issues below fall into the sphere of toxic parenting.

FAILING TO PROVIDE EMOTIONAL SECURITY

Emotional security is the measure of stability of an individual's emotional state and it starts in childhood. It's the foundation to all parenting. We've all heard about 'tough love'. Tough love in childhood is when children are treated harshly or sternly, and they're still expected to get on with and take care of themselves in later life. Conversely, when parents talk to their children about the things their children are concerned with, they become emotionally strong.

OVER-CRITICAL PARENTS

Some parents may be critical of their children, but whatever criticism is handed out, it must be constructive. It's easy for parents to become impatient: usually when their child fails to grasp something they're being told for the first time, and this can lead to being over-critical.

The odd time may be considered normal, but when a parent continually criticises and becomes overly critical without giving their child any credit, that's when parenting becomes toxic. It's also easy for parents to make the mistake of thinking that being overly critical is helping their children avoid costly mistakes, but any form of criticism if used regularly will cause a child to criticise themselves well into their adult years.

WORDS THAT HURT

Parents may get angry from time to time, but a parent's tone and language will define how their children respond back. When parents regularly use raised voices and words that instil fear into their children, their children will follow the same pattern. In a child's formative years, their brains are like sponges. What we tell them will stick and become their inner voice, therefore it's important we keep reinforcing positive words and actions.

Children need to be supported and feel loved so they will want to stay connected. A parent needs to change their behaviour if their child begins to feel threatened, fearful or scared.

Other toxic parenting behaviours might include:

→ Causing a child to justify his or her behaviour;

→ Parents putting their feelings before their child's;

→ Parents not allowing their children to express themselves;

→ Parents making toxic jokes about their child;

→ Parents ignoring healthy boundaries.

Children get used to the way they're parented, so they're not always consciously aware that their parents' parenting is, in fact, toxic. As an adult, if the way you've been parented falls into one of the above categories, then you've experienced toxic abuse. If parents don't want to change, children will emotionally distance themselves.

'I can't go back to yesterday
because I was a different person then.'

LEWIS CARROLL, *ALICE IN WONDERLAND*

BEYOND THE BLAME

As adults, how many of us will continue to blame our parents for the way we've turned out? It's obvious why we may point the finger and in some cases it's justified, but how long can we continue to blame our parents for our misgivings, without taking back some form of control for ourselves?

Many of us have been hurt, emotionally, psychologically and physically, and that's totally unacceptable, but to continue to blame our parents is to deny ourselves the chance to leave our past behind and be at peace.

The more we blame, the more we live in denial and living in denial, not choosing to take responsibility back, will only hurt us more. And even though we may have reason to blame our parents, it is more beneficial for us to move on. As adults, our lives must start being about us.

Not letting go means that over time we will begin to lose our sense of reason, our sense of hope, our sense of optimism, and that will destroy any future potential we have. When we can let go of anger and resentment, when we can begin to understand ourselves and our experiences more, we can begin to rebuild our lives.

We must use our experiences as a stepping-stone, so that we change our children's lives too and our relationship with them. After all, when our children become adults, would we want them blaming us for their misgivings?

THE HEALING PROCESS

When we can accept people's bad points as well as the good, we know we've worked through a process of understanding: when we can continue to have a relationship with the people who hurt us and are willing to let the hurt go, we know we've worked through the healing process.

When we can also begin to move forward without holding back or getting angry, we know we've worked through the healing process. When we're calm, and things generally don't bother us any more, we know we've worked through the healing process.

It's important to have positive perceptions and an understanding of the bigger picture of our experiences because those practices will help with the healing process.

COMING THROUGH ABUSE

There are still times when I can't believe that I've had to deal with neglect and trauma. I also didn't know that growing up with no emotional support, not knowing about my disability, not being able to talk about my feelings around a disability I didn't know I had, and emotionally having to pull myself through each day, was continually being etched into my psyche.

As my emotions continually spiralled out of control, the neglect and trauma finally manifested itself in anger. It is our families that must realise, understand, and want to help.

I know that without these experiences, I wouldn't be writing and I reconcile. But we don't just get over neglect or trauma, it's something we must continue to work on. Experiences become lessons, but for the healing process to work, we must put physical and emotional distance between us and those who have hurt us.

Recognising neglect or trauma is one step forward towards healing. But having to constantly defend ourselves in those circumstances, or having to be on our guard, means we're tied to unhealthy patterns, including control and submission: and being on the receiving end of that will continue to stay with us.

To recognise that we're not to blame is very much a mental-health step forward. To understand that we have the power to change how we think, how we feel and how we act is also another step forward on the road to recovery.

It is important we begin to recognise how people's behaviour manifests, because it is through our recognition that we get to see the bigger picture around our circumstances and what we have to deal with.

It is important to accept what happens, because without acceptance it will be difficult to move on, but we must remember that other people's bad behaviour isn't about us. It's about other people's inability to see their own worth and how they feel about themselves. On our part it is important we understand how they make us feel and don't make those feelings personal to us, because they're not.

Lamenting the past and blaming ourselves for not being able to change other people's patterns of behaviour is unhelpful and damaging, and simply reinforces where we are. If we could change our experiences around those patterns, we wouldn't be who we are through those experiences.

'A good head and a good heart are always a formidable combination.'

NELSON MANDELA

BEING ACCOUNTABLE

Being unaccountable means that we will never take responsibility for ourselves, or our actions. It also means we'll continue to apportion blame and find excuses, put things off and indulge in only doing the minimum.

Accountability is the total opposite: accountability is taking responsibility for all our actions regardless of the consequences. If something goes wrong, we are accountable. But how many of us would rather plead ignorance than take responsibility and be accountable for what we put out there?

We find it easier to say, 'I didn't do it,' 'It's not my job,' or 'I didn't know,' rather than accept accountability. Many of us, disappointingly, are accountable only when we know we're not going to get into trouble, or be penalised for something we've done.

Children often seem to be the worst culprits, but if parents don't teach their children accountability, they will never be accountable as adults. The less accountable we are, the more we will take a back seat, we will never be to blame even if we are, and we will always pass the buck to someone else. When we're not accountable, any white lies we tell will always turn into more serious ones.

Being accountable is important and is the right choice to make. It's also part of the healing process because a change in attitude will always promote emotional growth.

A LEVEL OF ACCEPTANCE

I believe we must find a level of acceptance in our experiences, regardless of what we deal with, because without an acceptance of any kind, we will remain mentally stuck.

When we learn to accept what we've had to deal with, we break the cycle. There will be things that we can change and being able to change those things will help us move into a better headspace, but that's not always an option we have open to us. Most things we deal with are brought about by our state of mind.

If we work on our state of mind, we can eventually come to reconcile. For some of us, we already know that we should reconcile, but a part of us still wants what we know we can't have. Since I was a little girl, I always knew that I was living with some sort of disability, even though I didn't know what it was, but there were times when it didn't stop me wanting to be the same as my siblings.

Being in a constant battle/struggle to accept our experiences can be emotionally and physically draining. It doesn't matter whether you live with something from birth, or something happens later that changes the way you look and feel about yourself, there still has to be a level of acceptability that you can work with.

There is a school of thought that says if you're born with something it should be easier to live with, because you don't know any different. To some extent that's true, but the flip side is that it doesn't stop you wanting what others have.

For me there isn't a right or wrong way of thinking. It's down to us as individuals. No one has a monopoly on what we think, in the same way we don't have a monopoly on what others think. I have days where I find a certain acceptance and everything feels easier, then other days when I wake up with the burden of what I deal with.

CHANGING OUR BEHAVIOUR

I have always been fascinated how, with a little understanding, we can change things. I want to elaborate more on how when we work towards changing the subconscious, we will change the conscious and as a result we will change.

The subconscious the key to maintaining a positive attitude. The conscious mind decides what we want to do, but ultimately, it is our subconscious that tells us what we will do. When we consciously choose to do something, we are simply trying to achieve our goals and dreams through our present thoughts.

We may start off with good intentions, and even decide what goals we want to achieve, but it's the old beliefs and habits that are stored in our subconscious that stop us from reaching those goals. By changing the thoughts that come from our subconscious mind, we can develop a positive attitude; for instance, we can decide to follow a healthy and nutritious diet, and we can change our beliefs and habits.

Different techniques can be applied to help us change our thought patterns and the entire thinking process. Once we have decided what we want to improve on or change, then we can go about achieving it. Certain techniques such as affirmations, visualisation, hypnosis and meditation can be used to help change our subconscious thinking.

Research has confirmed that it takes a minimum of thirty days to change our thought patterns, habits or beliefs. Consistency is one of the key factors in reprogramming the subconscious. Once we understand the processes behind the subconscious and conscious, we can change.

The subconscious and conscious need to work in sync with each other over an extended period for change to happen. Without that, we will go back to our old habits of thinking and behaviour. As part of the process, it is important we think about our lifestyle and deal with any past issues.

CHILDREN'S CONFIDENCE

Confidence is the backbone of our ability to function in our lives. There are so many things we will get wrong, when we lack the confidence. If parents engage their children when they're small, they will engage with confidence as adults.

Children may not understand how to articulate their thoughts with their parents in the early years, but they learn from us as parents, so it's important we teach them basic values such as saying please and thank you, being polite and courteous and having consideration for others. Those will all help build their confidence.

Positive feedback from us is vital and will help children continually re-assess where they are. Praise helps children's confidence grow without them being consciously aware that's what it's doing. Self-expression is something that children need to experience from an early age. Expression is necessary and should always be encouraged. Where a parent's mind is preoccupied, they will multi-task on their listening skills without giving children their full attention: but parents must try and change that.

When it comes to hobbies, we must want to take an interest in our children's hobbies. Hobbies are confidence building.

When it comes to criticism, if we're going to criticise our children for something they've done, it's important we make what we say constructive. Children believe the things parents tell them, so it's important to be specific and only refer to their behaviour.

WHY WE SHOULD ASK QUESTIONS

Children have a natural curiosity. They're keen to learn and understand, asking questions that will help them grow and function in their world. As adults, we're not all good at asking questions, let alone how best to respond to them.

When I was in school, children were mostly taught to focus on finding the correct answers to questions put to them, rather than ask their own questions, or explore their own understanding. But we can never expand our minds that way. Not being able to ask questions means someone else's belief system will become ours, and so the cycle continues.

Our belief system needs to be our own, so that we choose how we want to think. When we learn new things, we push ourselves beyond what we already know. We can still listen to other people's responses and opinions, but we need to be able to form our own.

Only then will we start to view the world differently. Seeing the world from a different viewpoint gives us opportunities to be encouraged and to ask more questions, so that we can challenge ourselves further. As a result, we may even get to make new connections along the way.

DIFFERENT PERCEPTIONS

It is fascinating that two people can be brought up by the same parents, but have such different, and conflicting, world views.

An object will always be the same, but each person's view of that object will be different, as will their interpretation. The way we view people will often determine the way we will behave towards them, which is why brothers or sisters will never see the world and their parents in the same way. It may sometimes work against us.

It is our personalities that make us different from each other: the way we think, feel and act, how we problem-solve, how we express ourselves. How we perceive a problem is usually the key to how we will solve it.

The way we perceive ourselves will determine how effectively we deal with our issues, our lives and our career choices. Perceptions form the basis of our attitudes, judgments, decisions and emotions. Perceptions may also turn us against each other, especially when it comes to siblings and families, but we should try to fight against that. Instead, we should use our perceptions as ways to be empowered.

When we come to understand that we all have different ways of interacting with the world, we can utilise that knowledge to create a more complete and empathetic understanding of ourselves and each other.

FULL OF HOPE

As a child, I always lived with hope. For me hope was positive, it was a faith, an innate belief that I would get through whatever I was dealing with, no matter what.

But hope is something we need to hold on to if it is to continue to work. It must be a fundamental part of our lives. Hope gives us access to all areas of our lives. It also gives us a reason to get up in the morning, it gives us a purpose, and can help us to reach our full potential.

Hope is a choice. We can choose to have hope, or we can choose to ignore it. If we choose to have hope, we believe that life will come good. That whatever the outcome, hope will still be there.

One way to increase hope is to be more mindful about what we deal with. Hope can spill into all areas of our lives. Having hope helps us focus. Hope gives us a quiet confidence that our lives will work out.

Hope helps us bounce back from setbacks and challenges more quickly. Hope allows us to believe in ourselves and in our abilities, where we would otherwise have given up.

It channels positivity and helps us not to revert to all things negative. It's that little voice inside our heads, telling us it's not time for us to give up.

'Yesterday I was clever, so I wanted to change the world. Today I am wise, so I am changing myself.'

RUMI

ESTABLISHING BOUNDARIES

Boundaries are a dividing line between what we can and can't do. They are what parents put in place to protect their children and other children they come into contact with. Boundaries are taught by parents to their children from a very early age.

All children need boundaries to keep them safe and secure, but some will push against their parents' boundaries, whereas other won't.

But boundaries aren't just for children, they serve adults too and are crucial if we are to build and implement healthy relationships. Adults without boundaries may be objectionable, and may also lack communication skills, because they've never learned how or what makes good communication. They may also act independently when making decisions without any regard for others. What one person who has grown up with boundaries thinks is appropriate, a person without boundaries may find totally inappropriate and vice versa. All differences must be respected.

Healthy boundaries are there to help us take care of ourselves emotionally and physically. They help us communicate safely and effectively without us overstepping the mark. It is the reason why boundaries are so important and why they should always be maintained.

CHAPTER 4

PHYSICAL HEALTH

'Physical health' has been defined as a state of physical wellbeing in which the individual is able to perform daily activities without problems.

In humans, a more helpful definition of health is this: our ability to cope with all of the physical, mental and social issues that we face on a daily basis, rather than the absence of illness as we might first think.

Disabilities are not one-dimensional – one size doesn't fit all – but no matter what we do, we must bring our disability and what we physically deal with into our mental thinking.

It's not something I always knew to do or did, because my disability was completely ignored, but the physical side to what we deal with has to fit in with how we cope mentally. Without being mentally strong, it will be difficult to deal with the physical.

PREVENTATIVE HEALTH

We cannot totally rely on preventative healthcare to keep us well. To say something is preventative means we can avoid that something altogether, and that can never happen in the way it suggests.

We cannot prevent illness. There are other factors that must always be taken into consideration, such as stress, hereditary conditions, emotional wellbeing, age and environmental issues.

There are things we can do to lower our risk of getting ill, but to think preventative health is completely preventative creates a false sense of security. Poor health can never be completely prevented, there are too many other factors we need to consider.

There are so many conflicting reports out there in the media about health and what constitutes good health. We are constantly bombarded with the latest medical theories. But we must take control of our own health so that we may reduce our risk of illness.

We need to be proactive in all our healthcare needs, instead of relying on others and the government to tell us how to live our lives.

EATING HEALTHILY

Heart health is so important, too important to neglect. We need to understand what helps keep the heart working at optimum level.

I know that being born prematurely is the reason I have difficulties with digestion and is why it's even more important for me to eat foods that are healthy and that agree with me. Being stressed also interferes with my digestion, but it's not always easy to know from day to day whether the problem is due to my being born prematurely, whether it's food related, or whether it is caused by stress, or a combination of all these factors.

When it comes to the heart, exercise can help us cut down on heart problems. Incorporating exercise into our lives at least three times a week is necessary. Certain vitamins and foods have also been shown to be beneficial. Vitamin B not only provides the body with energy, it is also good for the heart.

A lack of vitamin B, particularly B9 and B6, can lead to high levels of homocysteine (an amino acid in the blood), which may damage arteries, leading to heart disease and a stroke. Maintaining the right level of homocysteine in our blood is therefore very important.

Blueberries are an antioxidant superfood that go well with other fruit, or simply mixed with natural low-fat yoghurt and granola for the perfect snack. Blueberries contain an antioxidant called anthocyanin, which may help reduce our risk of heart disease. Blueberries may also help with the ageing process and in the reduction of certain types of cancer.

Eating fish is another good way to boost heart health. Oily fish contains Omega-3 fatty acids, which is beneficial in lowering blood cholesterol. It also has a positive effect on the heart and reduces cardiovascular problems associated with heart disease.

Foods that are high in fibre are also good for the heart, because they contain psyllium, a fibre that helps reduce cholesterol and keeps the heart healthy. Foods such as bananas, apples, pasta, broccoli, cabbage and whole-wheat bread are all good foods containing fibre.

There are connections between and consequences to everything we do, and diet is no exception. Everything should be taken in moderation. A little bit of what we fancy does us good emotionally, but we also need to continue to make sensible food choices.

We must educate ourselves so that we are nutritionally aware. Balance, moderation, being responsible and sensible about our food choices, helps us contribute to becoming more aware and staying healthy.

ISSUES AND ILLNESS

I have always known how important it is for us to deal with personal issues before the person we have an issue with is no longer around. Working through my father's illness taught me that. A few years after my mum passed, my father was told he had lymphoma. Because my spiritual beliefs were so strong I knew he would be OK, but I did struggle with the stress of having to work around his illness. My father would never admit it, but he wasn't the easiest of patients, the pressure was already on for us to take care of him.

I have never coped around illness, and now I know it has everything to do with my sensory issues. My being around someone with a terminal illness can create a visual stimulation that causes fear in me that's often hard to deal with.

I was more distraught when my mum was terminally ill than I was with my father's illness. I struggled to grasp the fact that she may not survive and I would have to see her deteriorate in front of my very eyes. I was also younger and my relationship with her was different.

It is only when a loved one is faced with a terminal illness that we realise how many unresolved issues we have, and coping with the illness is made more difficult if we haven't dealt with our issues. But unless we say something, it's too late once they're gone. It is important we speak our truth: to leave unresolved issues because we're afraid to say what those are, means we will continue to live with those issues long after our loved ones have gone.

If you have a close-knit family and have very few issues to address, it's perhaps easier. It's not something we're always lucky to have, particularly if you grew up in a household where you weren't encouraged to talk about things and show others how you feel.

Dealing with family members who don't talk can be difficult: even harder trying to talk about an issue with a family member who has a terminal illness, particularly if they're not interested and don't want to talk, or bring closure.

If someone doesn't want to talk about their issues before their terminal illness diagnosis, the odds are them being ill won't make a difference. When our parents don't talk about things, it can make it easier for us to understand how important it is for us to talk.

Thankfully, although I didn't manage to go into any great detail, I did manage to address my non-diagnosis. Now I won't look back and feel remorseful that I didn't say anything.

A good laugh and a long sleep are the best cures in the doctor's book.

IRISH PROVERB

STIMULANTS

Stimulants are drugs that increase activity in the brain, temporarily increasing alertness and energy. While they can elevate mood, they can also be quite addictive. Caffeine is a prime example of a seemingly harmless stimulant.

WHAT ARE THE PROBLEMS WITH CAFFEINE?

In the long-term caffeine becomes addictive, meaning the more we drink it, the more we feel we need to drink it. Caffeine may make us feel more alert and more energised as a short fix, but in the long term it means we can become addicted.

WHAT DOES CAFFEINE DO?

Caffeine blocks the receptors for brain chemicals, leading to an increase in adrenalin and alertness. The more caffeine we drink, the more the body becomes used to it, the more it becomes insensitive to its own natural stimulants.

This spiral continues as we become more and more reliant on it just to make us feel normal, resulting in the body's inability to produce its own natural stimulants and leading to an addiction. Feelings of depression, exhaustion, and an inability to cope without a regular consumption of caffeine usually follows.

But coffee is not the only product that contains caffeine. Caffeine is also used in the manufacture of Coca-Cola and energy drinks, including Red Bull. It is also used in tea. Green tea and chocolate drinks contain caffeine, but not in the same measure as Coca-Cola and Red Bull.

THE HEALTH RISKS OF RED MEAT

In a large US study reported in *New Scientist*, November 2006, that looked at the dietary intake of protein in almost 90 000 female nurses to explore their risk of breast cancer over a twenty-year period, red meat was found to be linked to incidences of breast cancer and also a number of other cancers, including bowel and colon. The study included 88

803 female nurses aged between twenty-four and forty-three, all from the US. These women had all participated in a wider study previously and had completed a questionnaire about usual dietary intake in the past year, in 1991. The researchers considered the findings from the 1991 questionnaire to represent dietary intake in early adulthood. The nurses then completed the same, or a similar questionnaire in 1995, 1999, 2003 and 2007.

WHAT HEALTH RISK DOES EATING RED MEAT POSE?

The main finding was that a higher intake of both processed and unprocessed red meat was associated with a 22 per cent increased risk of breast cancer. The results suggested that women who chose healthier sources of protein, such as chicken, nuts and lentils, had a decreased risk of breast cancer.

The main findings of the study were that:

→ A higher intake of total red meat was associated with an increased risk of breast cancer;

→ Higher intakes of poultry, fish, eggs, legumes and nuts were not associated with overall risk of breast cancer;

→ A higher intake of poultry was associated with a lower risk of breast cancer among postmenopausal women.

The study found that when estimating the effects of different protein sources, substituting one serving of red meat with one serving of nuts, peas or lentils a day led to a 15 per cent lower risk of breast cancer among all women.

Substituting one serving of red meat a day with one serving of poultry was associated with a 17 per cent lower overall risk of breast cancer. Also substituting one serving a day of red meat for one serving of combined legumes, nuts, poultry and fish was associated with a 14 per cent lower overall risk of breast cancer. (Source: https://www.newscientist.com)

It is important to note that this is only one study and needs to be interpreted alongside the wider body of current evidence related to dietary factors and cancer risk, so it is not yet clear whether additional research will lead to a different set of conclusions about dietary links with breast cancer.

It should therefore not be concluded from this particular study alone that red meat and processed meat increase the risk of breast cancer.

NUTRITIONAL HELP FOR ARTHRITIS

Arthritis is common in cerebral palsy. Arthritis is usually brought about through wear and tear on cartilage over time, resulting in pain and stiffness in the joints. Although cerebral palsy is not a degenerative condition, it does cause secondary conditions such as arthritis.

The pain experienced with arthritis can sometimes also be triggered by the food that we eat. To identify and avoid allergens, we must first test for allergies. The most effective test is called an 'IgG ELISA' test that takes a finger-prick blood sample.

Then there is the usual elimination diet challenge, which allows us to look for likely culprit foods by process of elimination for a two-week period minimum, whilst noting any changes in either our physical or mental health.

Foods are then reintroduced one at a time, leaving 24 hours in between each introduction, with any reaction to newly introduced foods closely monitored. Finding out what the culprit foods are may lead to less pain and inflammation.

Both tests should be done under the supervision of a nutritional therapist or someone who deals with allergies, so that the necessary support is given. They would also supervise a diet, that would compensate for the foods taken out because of allergens.

There are foods that may help reduce inflammation and pain. The best ones include:

→ Green vegetables: eating more alkaline foods such as green vegetables will prevent the build-up of acid in the joints;

→ Blueberries: contain anti-inflammatory properties that help reduce arthritic pain;

→ Ginger is also used as an anti-inflammatory that helps reduce arthritic pain;

→ Pineapple contains an enzyme called bromelain, which has anti-inflammatory properties. It is rich in vitamins and minerals. Bromelain also comes in supplement form.

Cutting down on or taking meat and citrus fruits out of our diets will also go some way to help alleviate pain and reduce inflammation. Eating oily fish three times a week is also known to help.

IBS, STRESS AND THE BRAIN

Some children with cerebral palsy can be prone to different digestive issues, including bloating, constipation and IBS brought about through an immature gastro-intestinal tract and sluggish bowel. Being born premature is known to be another factor.

We also know there is a link between IBS and stress. Now there is more evidence out there to suggest how they are linked.

Experts believe that IBS occurs when the delicate relationship between the nerves, hormones and electrical activity that link the bowel and the brain is disrupted.

Because of the connections between the bowel and the brain, it is now known that high stress levels can trigger IBS.

Pain sensors in the colon are more sensitive in a person who has IBS than in the digestive system of someone without the condition, and it is this that causes them to respond strongly to stimuli.

If you have never thought about a connection between the brain and the stomach, imagine the butterflies you get before making a speech, or the nerves you feel during a discussion that turns into a heated argument.

Now that we know the brain triggers the signals that cause IBS, it is up to us to limit the amount of stress we let in. It is also up to others to limit their stress, so that their stress isn't passed on to us.

INFLEXIBLE THINKING

There are people who genuinely live with difficulties in accepting change, shifting thoughts, making transitions and who demonstrate forms of inflexibility. Inflexible patterns will become part of us when we fail to demonstrate forms of flexibility. We know what we know and what we're comfortable with.

Inflexibility, or 'rigid thinking' as it's also known, comes about when an individual is unable to consider alternative thoughts to their current thinking, or are unable to consider different viewpoints and have difficulty finding innovative solutions to problems.

They will cling to their usual preconceptions and generalisations and may even react with hostility if they feel challenged in any way, or have to change their thinking. Past experiences around abuse or hostility may sometimes be responsible.

But it's not always abuse or hostility that brings about inflexibility. Bad parenting can also be the culprit. Children with inflexible thinking will become adults with inflexible thinking, who will base their beliefs on previous thought patterns that don't take into account new circumstances or new issues. New situations and changing circumstances are also responsible.

As we continue to rely on familiar thought patterns, we will miss new points being expressed because we're applying old thoughts to current circumstances. We may miss out on seeing the bigger picture. Relationships will become strained.

Those who deal with inflexible thinking will stick to the familiar and will never leave their comfort zone. Sadly, they will miss out on opportunities, relationships and experiences if they don't strive to stretch out of their inflexible minds.

'A wise man should consider that health is the greatest of human blessings, and learn how by his own thought to derive benefit from his illnesses.'

HIPPOCRATES

BRAIN FATIGUE

Brain fatigue is mental confusion that can happen at any time and without warning. When it happens it's easy to experience a lack of focus, reduced mental acuity and poor memory recall.

Although I was aware of some brain fatigue, I never really understood what it meant, or whether it applied to me, because I didn't know I had a disability.

I have now learned that brain fatigue is to do with how the brain is wired, in my case because I have cerebral palsy. If, like me, you feel like your head is stuck in a vice, you can't concentrate or function, or you just feel extremely tired, here are some practical suggestions below:

→ Cut out refined sugars, foods containing monosodium glutamate (MSG) and drinks containing caffeine. Eat plenty of protein and carbohydrates and cut down on saturated fats;

→ Eat lots of leafy green vegetables such as kale, spinach and rocket leaves and add some of the good fats too. Drink plenty of fluids;

→ Sleep at regular times so that you maintain mental clarity. Avoid exercising or watching television too close to bedtime as this will over-stimulate the brain. Being overtired can add to problems with mental clarity;

→ Exercise is known to reduce stress and encourage better sleep. It also helps us build up energy, so incorporating exercise regularly into a daily routine is an advantage;

→ Reducing stress is a vital part of a healthy routine and may help maintain mental clarity. It is therefore important to lower your stress levels and find time to relax;

→ Cut down on alcohol and smoking. The build-up of toxins from both these substances add to brain fatigue.

CHARACTER TRAITS

It is true that we all inherit character traits from our parents and spending time with our peers means we absorb theirs too, but what if the character traits we have are there because of a condition we deal with?

I was considered lazy at home and in school. It didn't matter how hard I tried, or what I did, I didn't manage to make the grades. No one talked about the fact that I was failing.

It was inevitable that I would struggle mentally, emotionally, physically and academically because of cerebral palsy and what I now know to be autism, but no one took the time to understand or ask questions that would help them understand 'me'; why I presented a certain way and what I had to deal with. Sadly, the things I struggled with didn't tie in with people's expectations of me.

Of course, some people without a disability will have traits that are annoying to others, but many of those traits are because of learned behaviour. For those with a disability like cerebral palsy, they may have certain emotional character traits because they don't have the capability to behave in any other way.

There are also many other conditions that have a similar effect, such as bipolar, memory loss, dyslexia, or any condition where the brain has been negatively affected in some way. It is very easy to make assumptions and fail to understand why people behave in the way they do. We genuinely need to stand back and be more accepting of people, particularly when it comes to disabilities.

Perhaps, we would also be much better placed to help others if we set out to understand, instead of assuming why someone presents in a certain way. We must ask and simply not assume.

OUR EMOTIONAL AND PHYSICAL HEALTH

The stronger we are emotionally, the better we will handle all that life throws at us. The stronger we are, the quicker we will bounce back from disappointments, and the better relationships we will build.

It is important that we learn to focus on our emotional and physical health as much as we can, so that we don't get lost in the complications of life. It requires as much effort to build and maintain our physical health as it does to build and maintain our mental and emotional health.

There are those who are emotionally and physically well and who have a sense of purpose. They manage stress quickly and efficiently: they have an air of contentment about them. They know what they want from life. They have the flexibility to adapt to new situations. Their self-esteem and confidence become second-nature. They move through life with a sense of calm.

In our busy and often stressful lives, it is important we all continue to strive towards better emotional and physical health.

SOCIAL TIES AND LONGEVITY

According to recent research, a healthy social life may be as good for your long-term health as not smoking.

Research was carried out at Brigham Young University and the University of North Carolina, where data was compared from 148 studies on health outcomes and social relationships from more than 300 000 men and women throughout the developed world. They found that those with poor social connections had on average 50 per cent higher odds of death in the study's follow-up period (an average of 7.5 years) than people with much stronger social ties. It's also a bigger factor than differences in the risk of death associated with many other well-known lifestyle factors, including lack of exercise and obesity. (Source: https://www.byu.edu)

In one of the most famous experiments on health and social life, Carnegie Mellon University exposed hundreds of healthy volunteers to the common cold virus, then isolated them for several days. The study showed that participants with more social connections and with a wider social network (friends from a variety of social contexts such as work, sports teams and church) were less likely to develop a cold than the more socially isolated study participants. (Source: https://www.cmu.edu)

In essence, the immune systems of people with lots of friends simply worked better, fighting off the cold virus, often without symptoms. Studies suggest that a strong social life affects immune function by helping people keep physiological stress under control.

As individuals, we are ultimately responsible for ourselves. There are so many other things we must take into consideration too. We must concentrate on our emotional, physical and spiritual health, because without those we will always struggle with our health. It is important to have friends and family around us who can help us, but we ultimately have to be able to help ourselves.

How we are spiritually and emotionally will set the tone for how we live our lives and how successful we will be. If we are happy within ourselves, we're more likely to have control of the things that go on around us: that means we're also more likely to get a better grip on stress and anxiety.

As time moves on, our lives will change and our children will move away. To give ourselves a chance of living longer and having healthier lives, we must be at peace with ourselves.

AN EARLY MEMORY

I have an early memory of looking in the mirror and checking the curves on my back. Even then I knew something wasn't right: when my shoulders were extended and straight, my back wasn't.

I would constantly stand and tilt myself around, so that I could see my back in the mirror. Although I had a slight suspicion about the curvature, I dismissed it, because it had never been mentioned, so I assumed I must be wrong. But throughout my childhood, it was something I would go back to, then dismiss because it couldn't be right, could it?

Perhaps deep down I knew I was right, but I didn't want to be. Then at the age of twenty-five, at my last check-up with a new specialist, my father was told that I had mild scoliosis, as part of the leg length difference brought about through cerebral palsy, that at the time I still didn't even know I had. It was something else that was never mentioned in any of my medical notes.

CEREBRAL PALSY IN THE SUMMER

I sometimes feel as though I am controlled by cerebral palsy. How I would choose to live my life isn't how I get to live my life, particularly when it comes to cerebral palsy and the clothes I like to wear.

Dealing with my disability means I continually have to work around things like my wardrobe, which can make it difficult, particularly in the summer months, as my condition has to come first.

As a child, I hated wearing skirts because of the lack of muscle mass on my leg, on my left side. I wanted to wear open-toe sandals, and flip-flops in the summer like my sisters. I wanted to wear three-quarter length jeans with pumps. Instead I wore clothes that covered me up. I hated that.

I was given flip-flops to wear because my sisters wore them: but it was obvious I couldn't hold on to them. My parents either weren't coming to terms with the fact that I had a disability, or they wanted me to be the same. I remember telling my mum that I couldn't keep my flip-flops on and trying to hold on to a sandal was impossible.

My writing helps me to evaluate and bring an acceptance to a lot of my experiences, including my clothes. When I talk about the things I know I couldn't change, writing about them makes me feel better. I have learned to dismiss the guilt and accept that is how it was. I was never in a position to say how I wanted things to be.

HIGH BLOOD PRESSURE

It is far better to have low blood pressure than it is to have high. Known as the silent killer because its symptoms aren't obvious, around 30 per cent of us in the UK have high blood pressure.

If left untreated, high blood pressure can increase the risk of a heart attack or stroke. It's something that should be checked every five years.

If after you've had two or three readings and your blood pressure measures 140/90 or higher, you are said to have high blood pressure (also known as hypertension). A normal blood pressure reading should be below 130/80.

Anyone with a family history of high blood pressure can be at risk, but as we age, our chances of having high blood pressure increase.

Other factors include:

→   Being overweight;

→   Consuming too much alcohol;

→   Being over sixty-five;

→   Consuming too much salt;

→   Not eating enough fruit and vegetables;

→   Not exercising enough.

To bring high blood pressure down to a controllable level, we must maintain a better lifestyle, introduce more exercise, consume less salt and cut back on alcohol. It's usually a poor lifestyle that triggers it. Anyone with a consistently high reading must be closely monitored, until their blood pressure is brought back under control.

Medication is not always necessary if high blood pressure can be controlled by a healthier lifestyle. A healthier lifestyle is something we should all be striving to achieve.

A doctor or other healthcare practitioner can advise.

CHAPTER 5

MENTAL HEALTH

Mental health is a positive sense of self and wellbeing, which allows us to function independently in society, in our relationships, and for us to meet the demands of everyday life. Having good mental health means we have the ability to recover more quickly from misfortune and illness.

Mental health has always been important to me. It's not the absence of illness or our emotions, but it is our ability to understand what our emotions mean to us so that we can use them to move forward in our lives, in positive directions.

My 'Mental Health' blogs incorporate all aspects of our emotions and how our emotions may present in everyday life.

GOOD MENTAL HEALTH

Mental health includes our psychological, emotional and social wellbeing. It is about how we feel and think as we go about our daily lives. Mental health determines the choices we make, how we handle stress and how we relate to others.

Having good mental health is brought about through a sense of self, self-esteem and confidence. It is important to have good mental health at every stage of our lives, from childhood, through to adolescence, and moving forward into adulthood.

The World Health Organization (WHO) says, 'Mental health is a state of wellbeing in which the individual realises his or her own abilities and potential.' When we come to realise our own abilities, we're able to cope better with the normal stresses of life, will start and continue to make positive contributions to our lives and will work productively. (Source: https://www.who.int)

According to estimates, only about 17 per cent of US adults are considered to have optimal mental health. Mental illness contributes to problems with behaviour, thinking and moods. Mental illness may be genetic, but life experiences can also affect mental health.

A family history of stress and abuse, both physical and emotional, can contribute to mental health issues. When interactions between the mind, body and environment begin to interfere and undermine our ability to cope with simple situations, then we know we're potentially looking at mental illness. Factors that contribute are acute or long-term stress, emotional abuse, drug and alcohol abuse, violence and family breakdowns.

Those with good mental health will automatically cope with stress and will continue to make meaningful contributions to their lives and to other people. They will realise and see their full potential. It is important for us individually to maintain and work on our mental health.

We cannot assume we will always have good mental health, but by choosing to connect with ourselves and others, we will continue to strengthen our resolve and perhaps at some point go on to help other people.

For those dealing with mental health issues including depression, it is important to try to develop coping skills, to remain in a familiar and comfortable daily routine, and to get enough sleep. It is also important to be physically active and talk about how you feel so that others are aware of your struggles.

EMOTIONS

Our emotions will either protect us or hurt us, but uniquely, what we all have in common are the emotional ties that bind us together, it doesn't matter what the emotion is.

As a child I was dealing with emotional issues. I wanted others to help me and take responsibility for my disability. I wanted others to listen, I wanted a voice. I just existed. I was frustrated, irritated and angry. When I wasn't angry, I wasn't happy, instead I was quiet, and when I wasn't all of those things, deep down I was the most kind and caring person, and those caring qualities are still with me today.

But no matter our circumstances or emotions, it is important we learn to remain positive, so that we can move on from just 'existing' in our lives. We will never make any positive contributions when we're just existing and being negative. But as we unconsciously continue to blame ourselves for the things that we've failed at, we're setting others free to continue with their lives.

It is important we learn to talk about how we feel. Talking about the things that matter or that bother us will give us peace of mind. Emotions are the most powerful tool we have. Emotions need to go somewhere: if they're not being expressed, they're being internalised.

By ignoring our emotions, they will eventually start to interfere with our health and this will contribute to long-term illness. The word disease is made up of two words 'dis-ease', which is why it's important for us to be at ease with ourselves.

EMOTIONS

CHANGING EMOTIONAL CONNECTIONS

We must shorten the divide between being told that we're loved and feeling that we're loved. That starts in childhood.

Unless we manage to clear the thoughts that prevent the flow of positive energy from moving freely through us, negative thoughts brought about by childhood experiences will be mirrored and recreated from experiences stored in our subconscious. We must learn to challenge and change our emotional connections.

As we continue to live our lives, our subconscious thoughts will continue to override our conscious thoughts and past experiences will continue to shape what we think, how we see ourselves, how we perceive others, and how we behave.

But for us to free ourselves from our subconscious thoughts and our past, we need to deal with our past experiences. It is important we continue to be aware of our needs in the present, so that we don't continually revert back to the past. Continually talking about the past means we're living in the past.

When we can live in the present, and have dealt with our past, we will form and continue to maintain deeper connections with those around us, which is when we will be at our most calm. We will feel loved.

REPRESSED EMOTIONS

When I think about my experiences, I still find it hard to believe 'my story' was my life; it feels too raw. It happened over a period of years, but those years could have rolled into yesterday, that is how raw it feels.

Learning how to handle our feelings is challenging. Our reactions may often depend on the situation and how we feel about those involved. As a child, I would angrily explode by negatively expressing my outward feelings to those in the firing line; those who I feel should have supported me.

For me to cope, there were times when I would mentally withdraw and build a wall around myself, and although it was never a conscious decision for me to retaliate, the nature of withdrawing also meant that retaliation would rear its ugly head at times. I know that my anger as a child was based on repressed and denied emotions around a disability I didn't know I had. It's a shame others never thought about that.

But however we get to where we are, it is important we learn to manage our emotions so they don't become a breeding ground for irritability and blame. It's also important we tune in to our emotions and deal with those. However hard our experiences are, we must learn from our experiences so that we can grow and take control of our lives.

TAKING EMOTIONAL CONTROL

The most important thing about our emotions is how we relate, connect and then deal with them. Taking emotional control is important if we are going to manage our emotions and our lives well.

However, when it comes to our emotions, it's easy to become distracted, particularly if we have more than one thing on our mind, so acknowledging our distractions helps. Working on our distractions will help bring any unaddressed emotions we have back into focus.

Our underlying experiences and beliefs will activate our emotions and how we feel. Therefore, it is important that we're aware of what those emotions are. What we tell ourselves works beyond any conscious reasoning, so we must start by correcting those.

The real emotional triggers are our unconscious thoughts. Although other people and events will trigger unpleasant feelings and reactions from us, they are not the only cause. It is important we own our emotions, but before we can do that, we must understand them. Without understanding, we may even deny our emotions exist or that they belong to us, let alone deal with them.

Taking emotional control is essential if we are to live well and have good emotional and physical health.

UNDERSTANDING MY FEELINGS

As a child, I was angry because I was aware I presented differently and there was no mental or emotional support in place. Things became more obvious to me as soon as I started school.

But it wasn't just about problems with school. Yes, those problems were there, but there were other issues too. I didn't understand my damaged brain, I also didn't understand I had sensory issues as part of my damaged brain.

From as far back as I can remember I always knew I had problems with textures. Certain materials didn't feel right. Certain knitted garments didn't feel right. I didn't understand why I was OK with some textures and not with others. Wire wool seemed to be a big no, no.

I didn't understand why things looked 'wrong' or why they didn't feel right, because they looked wrong. I also didn't know why I was anxious, or why I found it difficult to let go of issues: or why I continually had bad thoughts.

I also didn't know why I felt panicked when I wasn't in a routine, or why I panicked when I knew I was going to be late for an appointment, why I felt a sense of foreboding when things weren't familiar, or why emotional responses triggered a reaction of panic, as my thoughts and senses spiralled out of control. I wanted to know why and what exactly contributed to those feelings.

I also didn't know why I was unable to process what I heard accurately, or the delayed reaction to conversations, through my brain damage and sensory responses.

I still feel irritated that others see me as intense, stubborn and irrational because they don't think about what I mentally and emotionally deal with.

I know that what I went through is unique, but attitudes still haven't altogether changed around disability. There is still a nuisance factor, particularly in my case, when my disability was hidden and I had the resulting difficulties to work through.

OVERCOMING MY CHALLENGES

I had a tendency to give up on things as a child, and I never understood why until now, but that didn't stop others thinking I was lazy. There was a reason for my behavioural pattern, so that lets me off the hook.

Unfortunately, it didn't stop my flaws from being pointed out, which did very little for my self-esteem. I went through my childhood with my hackles raised, because of a lack of understanding of my neurological difficulties.

It's been a few years since my diagnosis was confirmed, and I am still finding things out about myself. Being a parent myself, it is a side to my life that I will never comprehend.

When I think I've found a level of acceptance, my subconscious tells me we're not done.

But now that I know why I have a tendency to give up, I can work to find ways to overcome it. My blog shows the world a different version of where I was all those years ago. I must continue to find ways to challenge myself, so that I can remain more focused and not give up.

My cerebral palsy and autism diagnosis certainly puts my struggles into context and helps others close to me to understand. They must understand it wasn't me being lazy: I had too many neurological challenges to overcome that continually got in the way.

REFLECTING ON MY PAST

I often take time to reflect on my past, as I believe it helps me pave the way forward. There will always be times when it's hard, but necessary.

I go back to not knowing about having a disability and remembering my struggles. Having to work through everything blindly was difficult and having to fight my corner, impossible. With no understanding and empathy, it was an endless battle: it was never-ending.

I believe reflection is a good tool to help us work through our past and family lives. It allows us to grow mentally and emotionally, helping us to look at our lives more positively, differently. When we can use our past as a tool without making the same mistakes, we will have learned our lessons.

141

Some benefits of using reflection:

→ Reflection helps us identify and learn from our mistakes;

→ It gives us a clear perspective;

→ A clearer perspective using reflection helps us change;

→ When we've mastered it for ourselves we can help others;

→ It can make us happier.

It's easy to look at our lives and feel guilty about what we've failed at, decisions made or missed out on, but that doesn't serve any purpose. It just creates more stress and irritabilities. Forced decisions that don't reflect our own thoughts or sentiments can and do make us feel guilty.

If issues become something learned and we can make future changes from them, then those issues will never be wasted. We cannot change the past, but we can change the way we look at the past. Studying the past is necessary because understanding certain aspects of it will help shape our future with new and better outcomes.

Without the past, we have nothing to check, measure and balance against. Any changes we can make from the past, although they may seem difficult or complicated, can result in new positive experiences and opportunities.

STANDING UP FOR ONESELF

As a child, I was a people pleaser. I used to go out of my way to please everyone. Although I believe it was the reason behind my search for acceptance, in hindsight I can see it didn't do me any favours.

What started as a kind gesture on my part became a habit to everyone else, because they knew I would never say no. What's more, it seemed contagious because it didn't stop with one person. I simply wasn't assertive enough.

Just because someone isn't good at saying no, it doesn't mean others should take advantage. It doesn't put those taking advantage in a particularly good light. I was continually being coerced into doing things, because I was too soft.

Things stayed like that for years, but I must have at some point unconsciously had enough, because as soon as I decided to change my perceptions, my attitude changed. For the first time I became assertive and things began to change.

It is our attitude that sets the tone on how things will go. The more positive and assertive we are, the less likely others will take advantage, and the more we will stand up for ourselves. And although confidence plays its part too, a permanent change of attitude is necessary.

As I began to reflect on my circumstances and the bigger picture, I began to perceive my experiences differently. Issues began to feel easier, I began to feel more in control of how I felt. My spiritual beliefs had a lot to do with the process, also. We must challenge ourselves to work through our own set of circumstances.

The new 'me' found a voice. If I choose to do something now I'll do it, just as I choose not to do something. I call my own shots.

The following suggestions may be useful to those who struggle with being assertive:

→ Express your feelings, even if your feelings don't concur with someone else's;

→ Say what you feel when you need to;

→ If others are capable of being responsible for themselves, you have a right to say no to taking on responsibility for them;

→ You are entitled to have your own thoughts and opinions;

→ You have a right to say no if what you're being asked isn't something you want to do;

→ You don't need to seek approval from others;

→ It's okay to have your own opinions and not allow others to dictate the way they see you.

Our life is for us. We have a right to be assertive, in the same way others choose to be assertive for themselves.

NOT STOPPING TO QUESTION

As children, we don't stop to question the decisions our parents make for us. We assume their decisions will be in our best interests, for our own good.

As parents, we can either make decisions for our children based on what we want, or we can make decisions based on our children's best interests. Early on in parenting and learning on the job, I came to understand how important it was for my children to be independent and free-thinking. It is important any decisions parents make are based on their children and not on what they want for themselves.

I am lucky in a way. Living with a physical disability as a child helped me see life differently. I spent my formative years continually observing my world. It wasn't something I could pinpoint or even understand at the time, things just felt different. It would take me another forty years to fully understand. Although I was never allowed to be independent, I was aware of how things should have been.

The inability of parents to let go of their children stems from their own insecurities; it's perhaps not something they ever stop to question but they need to. Looking back on my own life, I missed out on support and encouragement, which could have led to certain possibilities.

THE TRUTH

Always tell the truth, because it's the right thing to do. Telling the truth means we will never have to doubt and question ourselves, or other people. It also means we won't spiral into a world of deceit and it's good for our health.

With truth, we will have trust, but without trust we may never know whether we will have truth. It takes courage to tell the truth, particularly if we think it may hurt another person's feelings. When we don't tell the truth, non-truths will come back on us.

But not everyone is emotionally ready to hear the truth, and that's what makes our task difficult. It's not that what we're saying is wrong, but that what we're saying is not always ready to be received.

My mum always told the truth. She would rather hear the truth than be lied to, even if hearing the truth proved difficult. When we live without the truth, we're in denial of what the truth is. Telling the truth can make us vulnerable and open to criticism, but it's important to tell the truth anyway.

Truth and honesty are the epitome of life. It is what life should be about and is right because it fits in with what the universe expects of us. Truth forms the building blocks of our integrity and helps build the foundations for us to live with peace in our lives. It also helps with spiritual growth.

Having nothing to hide is much easier than hiding everything and getting caught out. Speaking our truth ultimately gives us the freedom to express and be ourselves, in a world where others may often draw comparisons with others. Instead, just be yourself.

MENTAL HEALTH AWARENESS

Good mental health is defined as 'a state of wellbeing', where each individual realises his or her own potential, is able to cope with stress associated with daily life, and who can work productively.

When we have good mental health, we will maintain good physical health. Without mental health awareness, we can never have full mental health. We must be aware and continue to make ourselves aware of the importance of mental health.

A brain injury that directly affects the brain chemistry can contribute to mental illness and can be the reason why a person with a brain injury might deal with a generalised anxiety disorder. For those who deal with a brain injury, it is even more important they seek help with their emotions.

When we consciously continue to make ourselves aware of mental health and we take care of any issues relating to mental health, achieving good mental health becomes easier.

MENTAL HEALTH AND OBESITY

There is a correlation between mental health issues and incidences of obesity. When we have mental health issues, it is not uncommon for us to overeat.

It's a fact that the Western world's population is becoming more obese. The World Health Organization believes that by 2020, obesity will be the single biggest killer. (Source: https://www.who.int)

Currently, it is estimated that at least 300 million adults worldwide are obese, with a body mass index of over 30. Compared to adults with a healthy weight, adults with a BMI greater than 30 are more at risk of hypertension, high cholesterol, stroke, heart disease, osteoarthritis, certain types of cancer and sleep problems. Over one billion people are overweight, with a body mass index of more than 27.3 per cent for women and 27.8 per cent for men. Obesity affects all ages and socioeconomic groups.

But the biggest reason for obesity is mental health. Recent studies have shown the link between obesity and mental health issues such as anxiety, post-traumatic stress disorder (PTSD) and depression. Other disorders that stem from mental health issues include binge eating disorder and night eating syndrome.

It is important that doctors address the underlying causes of obesity and ask the right questions regarding their patients' emotional health. Obesity is a symptom for which there is always a bigger picture, but no one ever makes the correlation: when we focus on our mental health, we can begin to cut down on obesity. Unfortunately, obesity has become a public health issue on an already overburdened system, but it's one that if not tackled at the root, may never decrease.

Unless those of us who struggle with the condition make the correlation, it's not something that can easily be fixed. Sometimes it's not always that straightforward, particularly if there is an underlying physical cause, like a thyroid problem. It may be difficult to start losing weight without outside help and guidance, but the root cause will always need to be addressed first.

Although obesity runs in families and is linked to mental health, our sedentary lifestyles, over-eating and a lack of exercise are all major contributors.

SELF-ACCEPTANCE

Self-acceptance allows us to let go of the things we cannot change. It allows us to identify our strengths and celebrate our accomplishments.

It also allows us to think positively and plan ahead. Self-acceptance allows us to take control of our lives, allows us to move on from the past and gives us confidence. Self-acceptance also empowers us to choose the life we want, so that we may find peace.

But to have self-acceptance we must deal with and let go of the past, because without letting go of the past, we can't live and accept new things. Self-acceptance allows us to focus and stay in the present moment. It also helps us to recognise our talents and capabilities.

However we get to do it, it is important we continue to be accepting of ourselves. We must look at our uniqueness, embrace and be proud of who we are.

MENTAL HEALTH AND ANXIETY

As a child, I didn't equate the bad thoughts I had with anxiety, or understand that anxiety was a mental health problem. It was a known problem that wasn't addressed.

We don't usually think about our mental health; instead we take good mental health for granted. Mental illness and anxiety is something someone else deals with, that we don't equate with ourselves. But it is important we all think about our mental health.

Although mental health and mental illness is different, not everyone will struggle with mental illness, but will have mental health. Mental illness refers to a wide range of mental health conditions that if left uncared for, will begin to affect our mood and the way we think. Mental illness includes anxiety disorders, depression and addictive behaviours, which if untreated, can spiral into mental health issues.

Mental health will always become a concern when ongoing stress and anxiety affect our ability to function. Mental health may turn into mental illness when the road ahead begins to feel difficult; when the issues we face cause us to question ourselves, and our mental state, and cause problems in our relationships, and in our daily lives.

In most cases, when it comes to mental health, therapy can help. Therapies help us manage the issues we need to address, by bringing a certain amount of understanding into the equation. Although medications help us cope in the short term, in the long term they suppress how we feel, rather than allow us to work out how we feel. It is important we are in control of how we feel.

Please get help if you or someone you know is struggling with mental health.

DESPONDENCY

Feelings of despondency can happen at any time, no matter how emotionally strong we are.

Below are suggestions for emotional, mental and spiritual healing of despondency:

→ Recognise how you feel emotionally, mentally and spiritually;

→ Take time out to reflect;

→ Try not to over-analyse but try to pinpoint where and why you may be feeling despondent;

→ As you work through the process remember to be kind to yourself.

The key is to allow yourself to feel despondent and own your feelings. Relax and rest until you're strong enough to move forward mentally. Always try to see tomorrow as another day for renewed optimism.

'No medicine cures what happiness cannot.'

GABRIEL GARCIA MARQUEZ

MY SENSORY PROCESSING DISORDER

Having cerebral palsy and sensory issues combined, means there are days where I struggle. I have the usual stresses made all the more difficult because of combined sensory issues. I will explain in more detail how Sensory Processing Disorder (SPD) interferes with everyday issues which those around me find non-challenging.

We all know about the five senses: sight, hearing, smell, taste and touch. My SPD affects four of those senses. The wiring of an SPD brain is different. These disorders are non-negotiable and don't present in the same way for everyone.

The best description I have read is by occupational therapist, A. Jean Ayres PhD (Source: http://www.otlondon.com), who likens SPD to a 'neurological traffic jam' in which certain parts of the brain don't receive the information needed to correctly interpret sensory information. For anyone who has SPD, if challenges aren't dealt with or met swiftly, it may cause panic.

With SPD we're constantly using our senses and where those senses happen simultaneously, all of which are vying for our attention, it's easy to feel irritable or emotional, particularly when we have too many sensory processing issues to deal with. SPD co-exists alongside most or all of my senses, therefore it's easy for those senses to become automatically heightened.

Any SPD issue will challenge an emotional response. For me it's always a response of irritation and panic as my thoughts and senses begin to spiral out of control and I begin to feel out of my depth. It's not easy for others to understand how I may present from one situation to the next.

For those who carry the burden of SPD, we're seen as awkward and irrational, making a 'mountain out of a mole-hill' on some of our issues, when in reality, we play hostage to issues that need addressing when they arise and can't rest until those issues have been addressed and mentally cleared.

Those without SPD have very little understanding of the disorder, but may still sometimes go on to form opinions. In the meantime, we must cover all angles just to get through the day and to avoid mental illness. It's a balancing act, not always easily achieved. I have to plan ahead, things have to be just right, or illness can set in.

For me, all the details relating to any issue I have, highlighted by SPD, must be ironed out and cleared up when they arise, so that I can begin to feel comfortable again, and to avoid the feeling of panic.

SENSORY ISSUES AS A CHILD

It is fair to say that I was never encouraged to think outside the box as a child. Not knowing about my disability or sensory issues kept me firmly in the dark. Everything unfamiliar feels daunting: through my writing I am now able to recall and place my experiences.

When I was a Girl Guide, camp was compulsory. I had no choice. I remember being driven to the drop-off point and my stomach was already in knots. Even before I got on the coach, the whole idea of going to camp filled me with trepidation.

When we arrived, I felt incredibly scared, so scared that my stomach was in knots again. I remember the feelings of panic, being completely out of my depth in a new environment. Emotionally, I couldn't cope: by tea time those in charge had already called my parents to come and take me home.

Camp didn't look or feel right and I put it down to being homesick. The open spaces made everything feel and look scary. In fact, everything about camp felt scary. I can remember those feelings as if they were yesterday. They are the same feelings I get when I work through anything new.

Since my diagnosis and for the first time, I am now able to explain and place my experiences with sensory issues. It feels good, if a little overdue.

TIME TO GROW

Depending on our childhood, each of us as individuals will grow differently. As a child, I didn't have a chance to emotionally grow because I was never encouraged to make decisions. Decisions were always made for me.

Although I was able to hold down a job from the age of eighteen, I didn't feel ready to 'take on the world'. It was only when I moved on with my life at the age of twenty-five that things slowly began to change for me. It was like being thrown in at the deep end without being able to swim.

I had to teach myself how to think independently, how to be independent and how to make decisions. As I slowly began to learn about myself, I began to grow and as a result was able to change certain aspects of my life. I found a voice in me that I never knew I had, and for the first time I started to look at my life differently. My focus and priorities began to change.

It is important that we learn perspective and allow ourselves space to emotionally grow. I believe in putting space between us and others when we have to. Having our own space is massively important, because it allows us time to renew ourselves with a more positive outlook.

BEING OPTIMISTIC

Being optimistic and looking on the bright side is important if we are to function and function well in our lives. Optimism, if continually sought, helps us overcome many hurdles, and whilst positive thoughts can be a cure in most cases, they must be coupled with realism to work effectively.

Optimism and positive thinking can improve our lives in many ways: having a positive attitude helps with our reality, and keeps the mind open and strong. Conversely, an attitude that is pessimistic and unrealistic may stop us from making important decisions, particularly around health issues.

Remaining optimistic allows us to explore possibilities around what we deal with, giving us a more balanced and hopeful understanding of our lives.

STAYING EMOTIONALLY WELL

How many of us find it hard to balance our emotions so that we stay at the top of our game emotionally and physically? Although we may try to stay emotionally well, some of the issues we deal with aren't always easy to get past.

My suggestions below may be helpful:

→ Make a mental note of your feelings. Try to work out why you have the feelings you have;

→ Always focus on the positive. It's a good way to stay emotionally focused. Focusing on the positive allows you to continue to attract positivity;

→ Physical health is important: take care of it. Try to exercise, eat healthy foods and get the right amount of sleep;

→ Stay connected with friends who elevate you, and who make you feel good about yourself;

→ Take up a hobby or find something that interests you;

→ Social networking can help you stay in touch with people you know, but don't always get to see;

→ Don't dwell on the things you have no control over. Keep past experiences firmly in the past. The focus must be on the thoughts you want to attract, so keeping your thoughts in the present is important;

→ Find your inner calm. It is important because without it, nothing else will work effectively.

We are more likely to handle stress, family and our lives better when we can achieve good emotional health. We are also more likely to be able to work through our issues and challenges with a clear head.

Making changes are never easy, but if we all managed to change just one thing, I believe it would go some way to helping us stay emotionally well.

AN EMOTIONAL VACUUM

No one's childhood is perfect. I am sure when we all look back there will be something we weren't happy with, or would like to have changed.

Having lived in an emotional vacuum for some forty-six years, it's something I'm finding difficult to come to terms with. Out of all my issues, this is the most difficult one to come to terms with. Until I learn everything there is to know about my disability, I am missing out on understanding all my symptoms and how they relate to a disability I knew nothing about.

Then there's forty-six years of having to adapt into a life that didn't allow me to live alongside a disability I should have known about. Having the support around my disability and neurological difficulties would have allowed me to work through and understand my struggles. I may have got help with school, instead of feeling I'd failed, and feeling isolated.

Growing up, I constantly lived in the dark: not knowing anything about my disability, about me, how to manage me, how to manage my life, and what made me, me. Out of everything I've had to deal with, those issues were always the hardest.

I have had to come to terms with many things, but I'm not sure how I'm supposed to come to terms with the enormity of not knowing I had cerebral palsy, how I presented, or what my neurological symptoms meant. Although childhood emotional neglect is what an emotional vacuum is, it hasn't stopped me from wanting to find out.

I could quite easily have given up. That thought did cross my mind on occasion. The emotional vacuum that was my life was in place for many years: it was my mum's terminal illness that opened the door to a new thinking on my disability. My life would then be changed for ever, in the form of a diagnosis and 'The CP Diary'.

WINNING THROUGH LOSING

From an early age, we learn from our parents and society how significant it is for us to win, but what it means to lose is even more important.

We can be prepared, trained, focused and experienced and still not win. Losing is an inevitable part of life, we cannot be winners all the time. Over a lifetime, we will lose more than we will win, so it is important we know how to deal with it.

Even if we lose, we need to recognise that we are all still winners. Finishing a challenge makes us a winner. Trying to win is a challenge, and overcoming any challenge also makes us a winner. Society should be embracing both in equal measures.

If a child in school finishes last in the egg and spoon race, there may be various reasons why that child didn't win and, although it doesn't feel good to lose, losing helps us to learn valuable lessons.

Like the stigma attached to disability, there is also a stigma behind losing: that perhaps a person is weak or didn't try, but it's OK for us to lose, we must be OK with it. Whether we come first or last we are all still winners. It is therefore our perceptions that need to change.

MY EMOTIONAL DEFICITS

Due to the nature of my cerebral palsy and the damage around my cerebral cortex, I know I am more mentally and emotionally disabled than I am physically.

The cerebral cortex controls both motor function and emotions, and in my case my motor skills and physical disability are relatively mild: the main issues revolve around my inability to feel emotions and my sensory issues.

There is no easy way to deal with a disability. Where one person might struggle, another with similar symptoms may not, but how we mentally think around our disability and the nature of what a disability is and how it can make us feel day to day, can make it hard for us to fit in. I don't think one element is harder than the other, I just think they're different.

I talk about my intuition a lot, because I use that as compensation for my lack of mental acumen. I use it in the context of my emotions and to gauge or anticipate how others might feel. I also use it to read other people's emotions and manage my thoughts constructively. I say thoughts, rather than feelings, because that is what they are. They're just thoughts.

The extensive damage to my cerebral cortex means I struggle with my emotional feelings, as they are impaired. Also, because of my autism it is easy for me to lock myself away. Inevitably I retreat into my own little world. My intuition acts as my guide and helps me work things out where my brain isn't able to do it.

I choose to adapt, to try to find acceptance with everything I deal with. Life becomes harder if I don't. I must fit my life around my disability, as others must try to fit into mine.

TAKING RESPONSIBILITY

When it comes to responsibility, we can apportion our baggage and discontentment to the events of our past where family is concerned, but that doesn't help, because we still have to function in the present. Instead, we must take responsibility for ourselves.

By the time we're adults, it's likely we've already stacked up a list of wrongs, assigning blame, but not taking responsibility for how we could have contributed to a more positive outcome. Having always tried to please others, I have now come to the conclusion that we must take responsibility and do what's right for us, regardless of what's gone before us.

When it comes to family, resentments, problems and injustices will sometimes surface, it's the nature of families; the consequences of which may mean we will drift apart. If that is the case, it's always best to try to sort out any differences.

IMPROVING EMOTIONAL HEALTH

For our physical health to work at optimum level, our emotional health needs to do the same. It is impossible to have one without the other.

But for us to improve our emotional health, we first need to recognise our emotions, and what they mean: we need to understand them. Once we sort out the causes of our emotions; like stress, anxiety and sadness, we will manage our emotions and health a lot better.

The following suggestions may be helpful:

→ Expressing your feelings is an important key to maintaining optimum health. Talking to someone you can trust is part of the process. If you don't have anyone you can talk to, a doctor could refer you on to someone;

→ Being able to relax and focus on yourself can help you to stay calm. A good method of relaxation is twenty minutes meditation or relaxation so you can focus on yourself;

→ Living a balanced life helps improve emotional health;

→ Keeping a journal of what's making you stressed or anxious is another good way to manage emotions. Seeing something written down can help bring about positive change;

→ Make time for the things you enjoy;

→ Take good care of yourself by eating healthy meals, take exercise regularly and avoid drinking too much alcohol.

Carrying emotional baggage will hurt us in the long term. Speaking our truth won't always make us popular, but it can bring about necessary change for us.

The truth will always open us up to other people's interpretation, but it can always be done in a conciliatory way that helps bring about peace. It is always important to say what you feel and what's on your mind.

'I've been walked on, used and forgotten and I don't regret one moment of it because in those moments, I've learned a lot. I've learned who I can trust and can't. I've learned the meaning of friendship. I've learned how to tell when people are lying and when they're sincere. I've learned how to be a teenager, and how to grow up when I need to. I've been to hell and back a few times, and I won't ever take what I have for granted. This is life, live it one day at a time. You never know how many days you've got left.'

UNKNOWN

WHY SUPPORT IS IMPORTANT

I have never made my lack of emotional support as a child an issue, because in my mind I was self-sufficient: I got by. But it is because of my lack of support that I know how important it is to have support and be a support to others.

Children will depend on their parents and family to protect them and to provide for their needs. But being a support doesn't mean we should try and fix other people's problems. It simply means we need to be a good listener and have a caring manner. We also need to make sure we don't judge, even if we don't agree with what someone else says.

Although support is a fundamental need for us all, it becomes much harder to maintain when one person is dealing with physical or emotional issues and the other must understand and act as a support.

How we choose to support is the backbone to all good relationships.

My suggestions below may help:

→ Take an interest and try not to criticise;

→ Listen to hear, not just to answer;

→ Don't make your opinion bigger than the person's you're trying to help;

→ Be conciliatory even if you don't agree;

→ It's not for you to decide what others should do, they must make their own decisions;

→ Body language is important. Be careful not to show how you feel, even if you don't agree;

→ Give the other person his or her own space: you don't need to know everything.

Relationships cannot survive well without good support being in place. But to have that we must first be able to listen.

Support should always be given in a caring and nurturing way, so that others don't feel compromised. It is an important part of the infrastructure that makes up a loving and caring family.

CHANGING OUR THINKING

I believe in the 'universal laws', so the sayings 'like attracts like' and 'what goes around comes around' resonate with me greatly.

Universal laws are the basic principles that rule every aspect of our lives, and are the ways by which our world and the whole cosmos works. When we begin to focus on positive thoughts, we will bring positive results back. Conversely, if we focus on negative thoughts, negative thoughts will come back.

As we learn more about the universe and its laws and how those laws can help us more adeptly, we will worry less about things. Changing any type of thinking comes through our understanding. Because the universal laws apply to everything we do, it is to our advantage to use and act on them in perfect harmony with each other.

PROTECT, DON'T SCAR

It is a parent's job to protect, not to scar their children. Some parents may have good intentions and set out to protect their children, but may end up scarring them instead.

Cross words, raised voices, negative tones all create emotional scarring if they are continually being used. When we use sarcasm, lash out, use words that attack, undermine and pull down, the patterns and scarring will continue.

As parents, we must make ourselves aware of how we communicate with our children at every stage, because it is in the early years where emotional scarring begins. If children have emotional scarring in their childhood, they will carry it into their adult years.

When any child is scarred, it is important they learn to focus their attentions on developing self-love and self-confidence. It is also important they love and validate themselves, instead of trying to attempt to win their parents' love, or vie for their attention, because in my experience that never works.

BOOSTING SELF-ESTEEM

There are many facets to self-esteem. Children's brains are like sponges, absorbing as much information as they can. The messages they receive eventually turn into self-statements. Their beliefs, attitudes and thoughts become ingrained, and turn into a part of them that isn't always accurate, but is accepted as true facts.

Other people's reactions, particularly from parents, shape a child's sense of self-worth. Any negative reactions they have will become stumbling blocks and that creates low self-esteem.

There are things we can all do to help boost low self-esteem:

ACCEPT A COMPLIMENT

It is hard to accept a compliment when you've never been paid one. Compliments must be felt: they're not simply words. Instead of dismissing a compliment outright from someone, accept and acknowledge to yourself the fact that they wanted to pay you the compliment.

AVOID LABELS

This is a common problem for a lot of people. But try to avoid pulling yourself down by saying things like 'stupid', 'lazy', 'can't', 'should' and 'never', and instead introduce words that renew your confidence, like 'I can', 'I shall', and 'I will'.

MAKE SELF-ESTEEM UNCONDITIONAL

Change your inner voice and embrace yourself uncon-ditionally by facilitating a more compassionate attitude towards yourself. Take away thoughts like, 'I'll like myself better when' and replace it with thoughts like, 'I like myself now'.

WRITE YOUR THOUGHTS DOWN ON PAPER

What we write down can become a self-help tool and is the first step to noting our internal dialogue: internal dialogue can always be changed. The changes we incorporate into our life should be small but significant ones that happen over a period of time.

There will be lots of days where we feel we're not achieving anything, but each significant step means we will become mentally stronger.

Try not to torment yourself over the things you feel you've failed at. A parting thought on this particular topic: perhaps it's not that you've failed, perhaps those things were never meant for you.

BEING HAPPY WITH ONESELF

When we struggle and think about others, we may think they have their lives pretty much wrapped up. We may look and focus on their qualities, rather than on our own.

From the outset, we may think their lives seem to fit together perfectly, but inwardly they will also have their own stories to tell. Instead, we must focus on our own qualities.

These are my own techniques to achieve happiness in oneself:

→ Never look at the past as something negative. Look at it as something you can learn and grow from;

→ Stop trying to please others, if pleasing others doesn't please you;

→ Being around people who intimidate you can make you feel worse about yourself. Instead choose to be around positive people who elevate you and who make you feel good about yourself;

→ Try to find ways that work for you so that you can take control over how you feel;

→ Don't worry about what other people think. Accepting yourself is easier when you ignore other people and what they think of you.

When you put a more positive spin on your life and your own qualities, you will be less inclined to question yourself. So, accept yourself, forgive yourself, and eliminate toxic people from your life. When you're happy with yourself, you won't want to be someone else.

'With the realization of one's own potential and confidence in one's ability, one can build a better world. According to my own experience, self-confidence is very important. That sort of confidence is not a blind one; it is an awareness of one's own potential. On that basis, human beings can transform themselves by increasing the good qualities and reducing the negative qualities.'

THE DALAI LAMA

BEING DIFFERENT

As a child, I wasn't aware of what my physical, mental or emotional difficulties meant, so I never understood why those difficulties made me different. I was only aware there was a difference in my leg mass and foot.

As children, we normally attune ourselves to people's appearances more than adults. For example, if a child sees another child who is overweight, that child will say something like, 'Look, Mum, that girl's fat.' I'm not really sure what my peers saw or thought about me, but however they saw me, I somehow adjusted.

My suggestions below should help us adjust to being different:

→ Believe in yourself. Use your uniqueness to move around your life. Don't let the fact that you are different hold you back. Being able to work through and overcome your difficulties will not only inspire you, but will also inspire others;

→ Stay positive, you are okay as you are;

→ Spend time thinking about and working through your challenges without homing in on other people's opinions of you. Certain challenges can always be overcome, it's the attitude that matters;

→ Choose to have people around you who support you unconditionally.

As individuals we are all unique, but those who have a disability and are different are even more unique and that in my book is OK. Society needs to embrace and celebrate people who are 'different.'

My disability and being different has taught me about humility, it has taught me about expression, it has taught me about resilience, and to recognise other people's struggles. It has taught me about tolerance, patience, empathy and compassion. It has taught me how to be a better person. It has also taught me about the importance of being kind.

BEING RESILIENT

Through my difficulties as a child I must have been resilient, because no matter how hard things were, I was determined to come through.

When we are resilient, we don't see failure as something to dwell on, but as an opportunity to learn. We accept that to fail can sometimes be part of our journey. Being resilient helps us bounce back, so that we can go on to make different and better choices.

I believe resilience comes from within us, from our environment, our peers and our schooling. A significant influence or event can also have a large and lasting impact that will test our resilience. My story has taught me that.

Resilience also teaches us determination, it teaches us how to cope when things are difficult. Once we have resilience, there is nothing we cannot do.

COPING WITH CHAOS

It is often the case that when our life is thrown into chaos, we manage to find ideas to help us work through it.

Feelings usually associated with chaos, such as stress and anxiety, will slowly begin to dissipate as we become more skilful at handling certain situations. We must make sure we continue to stay healthy through the process.

Once we are able to stand back, assess and observe how we might react better, we will cope better. But chaos and change are both necessary and, if utilised positively, can help us learn how to manage our lives more successfully.

When we look at a situation objectively, we will begin to understand more of what we need to do to transform our ideas into possibilities and to cope better. It's not always easy to know which thoughts or ideas will work, but drawing on our experiences and using our intuition will help us reach the necessary conclusions.

With experience, chaotic situations can be easier to deal with. When we find things easy, we will spend less time thinking about and working through those things. Each situation is different and must be assessed separately. Of course, we will never really know how we will cope until we're there.

CLARITY

Clarity is an understanding we achieve about something we previously failed to understand. It is what we create for ourselves. But to have complete clarity, we must avoid other potential thoughts that can veer us off course. It also doesn't matter if we don't have clarity straight away, as long as we actively work towards it.

Achieving clarity is difficult when we're dealing with emotional issues, or we're feeling tired or drained in some way. Life can run smoothly with everything working out as we plan, and then we meet a dip in the road, we lose focus and we need to rethink.

But we must continue to deal with life and all that life throws at us, and that can be difficult sometimes. When we are mentally tired we have less clarity. To have peace of mind we need clarity. Keeping an open mind on our issues and accepting we can change our thoughts can work: that we don't have to stay where we are.

Being able to understand and see other people's point of view also brings about clarity. It also very much depends on other people's approach and how they interact with us and what their intentions are. It is our understanding that brings about clarity. Taking out all the non-important things we're stressing about helps.

When we deal with things individually we can have clarity, because we focus on that one thing. With clarity, our mind can be at peace, centred and balanced. Whichever way we turn, it's important we feel calm and in control.

Through clarity we may bring solutions and conclusions to some of the issues we have to deal with, but we need to actively take steps to make it happen. As with most things, clarity is a work in progress.

WHY WE SHOULD REMAIN UPBEAT

Even from a young age, I always tried to remain upbeat no matter what I was dealing with, but remaining upbeat hasn't always been easy for me.

Part of the problem is that we come to accept where we are and see where we are as a *fait accompli* and that's usually how things stay, but the more we work on positive thinking, the more we will become resilient and remain upbeat.

Challenges can be difficult, but we may find they encourage positivity, which show us possibilities if we persevere. The better we are at working through challenges, the more positive experiences we will have, the more positive we will become and the more challenges we will overcome. The more positive we are, the more successful we will be.

Even highly negative people can rewire their brains so they focus on more positive thoughts. It is still possible to maintain an optimistic outlook and remain upbeat, even when the odds are stacked against you.

Tackle your goals step by step. That way you're less likely to feel overwhelmed, stay more positive and remain more upbeat.

SIMPLIFYING YOUR LIFE

I have noticed that in general society has become more materialistic. We want more than we can afford to have, own or need. We buy too many material things: whilst some children have more now than our generation had, more than our parents' generation had, they seem less happy than we were.

Some ways to simplify your life:

→ Make peace with your past;

→ Let go of the things you cannot change and change the things you can;

→ Stop holding on to anger and bitterness;

→ Cut down or cut out the relationships that leave you emotionally drained;

→ Relationships should be equal. If they're not, then it's time for a re-think;

→ Downsize your to-do list. Spend time on your own. Go for a walk, read a book, or listen to classical music;

→ Remember to say 'no' once in a while without feeling bad about it.

As a child, I wasn't indulged, primarily because my parents couldn't afford to buy me things. I'm pleased I wasn't. Life was more simple back then, more than it is today. Playing ball in the back garden when I was growing up was considered fun. That really was the simple life.

'The first step to becoming a more peaceful person is to have the humility to admit that, in most cases, you're creating your own emergencies. Life will usually go on if things don't go according to plan. It's helpful to keep reminding yourself and repeating the sentence, "Life isn't an emergency".'

RICHARD CARLSON

HAPPY AND CONTENT

People with happy dispositions will have periods of low moods, disappointments and problems, in the same way people who have unhappy dispositions will. The only difference is that happy people will adapt more easily and their disappointments and low moods will be dealt with more swiftly.

Happy people have a more relaxed and calm demeanour about them, regardless of what they deal with. They are more content in themselves and know to take the rough with the smooth. They're ready for what comes their way.

They are aware of how they feel at any given point. They accept the inevitable and will take things in their stride. They tend not to panic and know that as their low moods come, they will go. They seem to be more accepting of their feelings and aren't particularly fazed by what they deal with. They get on with putting their world right.

We must be content and happy within ourselves. We can work at being happy, but we must learn to adapt into a better lifestyle and work on our personal beliefs. All of our experiences are etched on our souls, so if our souls are tormented, we will never be happy, but we can work on change. Our beliefs and experiences can help shape our ability to stay focused and calm. Our experiences in turn shape our personality and our ability to deal with issues with some ease.

It is important not to fight your feelings and accept that you have them. Feelings are there for a reason. It is important you acknowledge they are there and learn to go with the flow, because that will help you become more calm and at ease.

REGAINING OUR PERSPECTIVE

Living with a disability I didn't know I had, together with my inhibited upbringing and knowing I struggled mentally, emotionally and physically, always made me feel like I was treading water, going nowhere fast. It was easy for me to lose my perspective on what I was continually having to deal with. I was agitated and angry most of the time.

Dealing with any kind of trauma can make us feel like that. It may be something we blank out for a while, a kind of coping mechanism.

Below are some steps to help deal with trauma:

→ Acknowledge what happened to you happened, and give yourself time. You'll never move past the setbacks if you don't manage some form of acknowledgement;

→ Put your setbacks into context. Although a setback can sometimes reverse progress that you've made, something you've tried to have a go at but not yet managed to complete; try not to see that as something negative. We learn from our setbacks, that was then, this is now. It can either be an ever-present part of your life, or something that was fixed, but something you can now draw inspiration from. We can always choose to think about our setbacks differently;

→ There is always something positive that comes out of something negative. It's not always clear at the time, but when we look back it can become obvious;

→ Sometimes you're just in the wrong place at the wrong time. If the situation was out of your control and there was nothing you could do, let it go;

→ Get out of the house. Going out is a good tool for breaking the habit of exclusion and being in a rut;

→ Exercise is known to release a 'feel good' hormone, go for walks to clear your head;

→ Think about one small change that will help you clamber out of your emotional rut;

→ Being proactive helps change your mindset even if it is only for a short while.

Being mindful allows us to be drawn into understanding our trauma. Once we understand, we can begin to quantify the enormity of our situation and deal with it. Once we're able to deal with it, we can then take back some form of control.

I believe it is only through our understanding that we will find a way to regain our perspective: that allows us to move forward through our trauma experiences.

TACKLING OBSESSIONS

If allowed to continue over a period of time, negative thoughts and feelings can turn into obsessions. Obsessions can be brought about through painful childhood experiences and traumas that aren't dealt with. It is important we look at, think about, and understand our experiences and how those have made us feel. We have got to be able to cope, and move on with our lives, therefore it is important we deal with all our experiences, past and present. Taking baby steps helps makes what we deal with more manageable and achievable.

It is important we try to limit the stress and anxiety our obsessions cause, because stress and anxiety will always make them worse.

So that we can tackle our obsessions, it's important we expose ourselves to them, because that helps us challenge any fears we have around them. We must subject ourselves to the fear we feel and work through the challenge. Although it's important we distance ourselves from the source of the obsession, it's important we deal with the obsession.

Learn to live in the moment, but first deal with the issues you've not dealt with. Focus on the things you've neglected and also try to keep the people around you positive. Facing your demons will always be difficult. In the beginning you'll probably feel uncomfortable, you'll want to back off, you may even feel a little panicky, but those feelings will dissipate the more you stick at it and work things through.

You must 'feel the fear and do it anyway'. Even if you take one or two steps back before you move forward during the process, one small step at a time will help you feel less anxious and more in control.

Keep a journal of your obsessions, put the obsessions that cause you less anxiety at the bottom of your list, with the more pressing and challenging ones at the top.

Take the first obsession and begin to practise working through it, until you notice you're feeling less fear. To break the cycle, you must fight any urges that tempt you back in and not give in to your obsessive tendencies. The important part is that you're finally getting to the point where you're beginning to feel comfortable around tackling your obsessions.

WHY WE SHOULDN'T CONFORM

I used to feel guilty because I felt I should have been stronger, instead of always conforming to how others wanted me to be. Now I feel compelled to write from my own viewpoint why I think it's important for us not to conform to other people's ideas if it's not right for us, and why we should learn to follow our own path.

It stands to reason that if we live by our own values, we will live a more peaceful life with less stress in it: to live by our own principles and be free to make our own decisions.

Instead, when we conform to fit into another person's beliefs, we live by their rules and not our own. But if what others are asking of us doesn't fit in with our plans, we must make our own decisions on what we want to do. When we try to match up to other people, it usually means we're trying too hard to find a level of acceptance from them. We shouldn't have to match up to others; instead we should celebrate who we are and our differences.

We must be comfortable around our non-conformity. Not conforming helps us grow emotionally, physically and spiritually because we're free to do our own thing. Try not to care about what other people think. You'll stop conforming, and as long as you're not rejecting other people out of spite, no one should make you feel bad.

It's your life to do with as you please, as others' lives are for them. No one should make you feel bad because you choose not to conform.

PUTTING YOURSELF FIRST

As a child, I cared about everyone and everything, regardless of who cared about me. I cared about what other people thought of me, so much so that I became influenced by their suggestions, even though their suggestions weren't always right for me.

I'd speak and say things to please and gave no consideration to my own voice. I cared too much about 'doing the right thing'. In hindsight, I should have cared more about myself. Now I think differently.

By all means care for others, but put yourself first. Try what you want to try. Stop concerning yourself about the things you can't control and take control of the things you can.

Stop worrying about the mistakes you make. Mistakes teach us important lessons about ourselves and about life. The biggest mistake most of us make is not doing anything, because we're afraid of getting it wrong.

Experiences teach us who we should care about. You'll know when it's right to care, because you will see others care about you. Your efforts will be reciprocated.

'When you find peace within yourself,
you become the kind of person who can live
at peace with others.'

PEACE PILGRIM

EMPATHY

When we can understand someone's feelings from their perspective and don't stand in judgment, we have the ability to empathise.

Empathy isn't something we're born with; it's something we can learn and practise, but it's not something we will all develop. To have empathy, we must put ourselves in another person's shoes and feel what that person feels.

Some of us have natural empathetic tendencies, whilst others don't. Some of us don't notice the feelings in others, while others simply can't be bothered to notice, but most of us will be somewhere in the middle and will understand in part how someone else feels. In the main, we tend to ignore how others feel when we're not coping well ourselves.

If our parents have empathy, we can learn about it from them. But even if our parents don't have empathy, there is no reason why we can't learn it. Empathy comes from within us, and from what we see around us.

Because I was a child growing up with physical and emotional difficulties, I innately understood how others felt. I learned very early on what empathy was. I could see someone else's suffering through my own suffering and that enabled me to easily relate.

We have to understand what others go through, we have to want to care and help others, to see things from their point of view.

It is important we have empathy. Society works better with it and although that relies on the greater good, when we use empathy, we will always get the best out of each other.

POSITIVE THINKING

If, like me, you were not encouraged to open up and talk about things as you were growing up, concerns, worries and problems will never have been discussed. That doesn't amount to positive thinking.

Perhaps our parents didn't talk about their concerns and feelings, so we learned not to talk either. Or perhaps it was because we weren't sure how our thoughts would be received, whether what we were saying was something our parents would think was stupid. But whatever the reason, if parents are open with us, we will learn how to be open.

We function better when we talk about things, and that helps give us a more positive outlook. Being able to think positively comes with many emotional benefits. Issues become less stressful and less stress means increased mental clarity. Those of us who continually think positively also experience better health.

Positive thinking is a great way of reprogramming the mind, so that we can tackle issues that crop up. But to deal with our issues, we must think positively and change any negative thinking. For us to practise positive thinking we must believe in the power of positive thinking, because that will bring about positive change.

THOUGHTS FOR POSITIVE CHANGE

A study by researchers at California University in 2010 suggests that by the time we're seven years old our characters are fully formed. (Source: https://www.livescience.com)

But what happens when we've had no support, when that voice in our head belittles our very existence, when it starts to draw comparisons with other people, and we become convinced by the negative things we tell ourselves?

We don't have to continually buy into it: we can change certain aspects and go on to live fulfilling lives, even without the early support. We can look at past experiences and situations, find new understandings and look for new emotional endings. With work on ourselves, we can bring a different thought process into the equation that helps change how we see and deal with things.

It is difficult to change the circumstances around trauma, but it is possible through continual work on ourselves to change the thoughts in our minds, so that we're not choosing to take in negativity from our past and other people.

HOW DO WE CHANGE?

We change by challenging our thoughts, and as we work through each experience as it happens, so that we're looking at the bigger picture, seeing everyone's part in the process and using our conscious mind to change our understanding.

We can't always change other people's behaviour in our past, but we can change the way we think and perceive their behaviour, by making the issues we're struggling with their responsibility, if they are responsible. The sad reality is that we don't; instead we carry other people's guilt when they choose not to accept responsibility for it.

We're tied to the thoughts in our subconscious and if they are negative we live negative lives. Bringing those thoughts back into the present, conscious moment and challenging ourselves to look at, understand and work through those negative thoughts will help us change our thinking. Also, as we learn to let go of judging ourselves and judging others, we can start to look at our issues and lives more positively.

CHOOSING TO THINK POSITIVELY

If we put out positive thoughts, we will get positive thoughts back: in the same way, if we put out unkindness, we will get unkindness back. Because the 'Law of Attraction' states that what we put out will find its way back to us, it is important we put out positivity and keep our thoughts positive.

By changing the way we think, we're paving the way for us to think positively; changing 'self-talk' from negative to positive.

Self-talk affects what goes on around us and how our mind interprets what happens to us. It also affects how we perceive and communicate with others. If we repeat self-talk often enough, the things we tell ourselves may become our reality. If more of us understood how 'self-talk' works, we would understand the need to be more mindful, because how we talk to ourselves and what we tell ourselves is a full conversation with the universe.

What we think about the most is what we're dealing with day to day. The mind starts out without negative or positive thoughts. How we talk to ourselves may define how our lives are shaped. That is why it is important to think positively.

MINDFUL THOUGHTS ON NEGATIVITY

It is always difficult to try to change our attitudes around our realities, because our realities are often so difficult to deal with. They take time to work through, particularly if we're living with negativity.

But mindfulness helps control negativity and is one of the most important skills we can have. Mindfulness is a mental state achieved by focusing our awareness on the present moment, whilst acknowledging and accepting our thoughts and feelings without judgment.

Mindfulness is the practice of concentrating on our breathing and noticing how our body reacts in that moment.

Being mindful is something we can do at any time, we don't need to be in a specific place to do it. It helps us learn how to detach from negative emotional thoughts, allowing us to create distance, so that we can respond and react more positively around negative or difficult situations.

What we should be aiming for is to observe our thoughts with little, or no reaction. Although it's not easy in the beginning, when mindfulness happens we can create a more neutral situation for ourselves, so that we're not homing in on negativity as much.

Being mindful has so many different positive benefits too. Being mindful helps us reduce daily stress and depression, and helps improve our immunity.

> 'Courage is what it takes to stand up and speak; courage is also what it takes to sit down and listen.'
>
> SIR WINSTON CHURCHILL

MY ANXIETY MANTRA

As a child, not knowing I had anxiety or why I struggled with bad thoughts meant I continued to deal with both. As an adult, I began to use a mantra to free my mind from bad thoughts.

My mantra, 'manah trayate iti mantrah', means a mantra which is brought to mind again and again. The mind has to *become* the mantra. The mind has to be *filled* with the mantra; once that happens the worry is taken away.

My spiritual beliefs have always been instrumental in how I see life, but because I live with anxiety and I must include my neurological difficulties as part of that, it is easy for me to go back to that place, particularly if I'm struggling with issues that aren't easily resolved.

I believe our lifestyle strongly influences how and what we think about; our lifestyle is also instrumental in us being able to take away any concerns and worries, so that we can live our lives more positively.

Negative or bad thoughts increase our fear and worry. Continually accessing those thoughts means you can find ways to change and move those thoughts away.

COPING WITH MY DEPRESSION

I wanted to write about depression from a personal perspective, because I believe I was struggling with it as a child.

Seeing anyone deal with depression now takes me back to my own childhood. I wasn't motivated, or interested in anyone or anything, and became withdrawn very early on. I don't remember a time when I was happy.

Struggling with bad thoughts, particularly at night time, meant it took me forever to get to sleep. My mum would often sit by my bed and try to calm me. When I finally found sleep my bad thoughts would disappear, but like a faithful friend those thoughts were always there when I woke the next morning. I never seemed to see the fun in anything.

There was no release. I was exhausted. There is a difference between feeling down and feeling isolated and withdrawn, and that is why I believe I was dealing with depression. I used to internalise everything. But slowly, I began look at things in its entirety, so that I would come to understand how I felt.

If you are feeling depressed, it is important to discuss it with your family doctor, with family or friends, or whoever you feel you can confide in. Always ask for help if you think you may be struggling with depression.

CHAPTER 6

LIFESTYLE, BELIEFS AND SPIRITUALITY

Lifestyle is how we live our lives. But to live a comfortable and stress-free lifestyle, we must also incorporate and work alongside our beliefs and spirituality.

Beliefs are important and are something that someone accepts as true or real, an opinion firmly held, but in holding our beliefs it is important we make sure we are also open-minded so that we can live comfortably alongside others.

Spirituality is not about religion or religious beliefs, but about our deepest values and the meaning by which we live. Although spirituality may include a belief in the supernatural (beyond the observable) realm, for me it's about personal growth, finding meaning through our own inner thinking, and values that we should be using in our everyday lives to make us more rounded and understanding as human beings.

Although I didn't know what being spiritual meant as a child, I always innately believed there was something bigger; an external force that worked in harmony with our inner thinking.

My 'Lifestyle, beliefs and spirituality' blogs explain and show how our beliefs and spirituality are intrinsic parts of our lifestyle. They go hand in hand. Even as a small child dealing with anger, I still had qualities such as compassion, love and patience. Being spiritual, I believe, offers us a sense of harmony, responsibility and belonging.

ROLE MODELS

Children are fortunate if they can look back on their formative years and embrace memories of a good childhood, with positive role models. How many of us can say we had good role models growing up?

I think a generation makes a big difference. Values, influences and society change through the generations. Outside influences bring change: both for the better and for the worse. But whether parents are good role models or not, what children learn stays firmly etched in their psyche.

Teachers will also influence children, as will grandparents: people we hope will positively influence our children. But there will always be people who don't make good role models, from families and institutions alike.

When it comes to parenting, we get one shot at making a difference, although we won't know whether we've been successful or not until our children are older.

THE NEED FOR PATIENCE

We live in a world where many people expect instant gratification. In the blink of an eye we have the information we need at our fingertips, through the internet.

We don't have to write drawn-out letters to communicate with family or friends any more. If we have access to a computer we can email, quickly and efficiently. Through technology we have moved forward.

Technological advances are positive, but the flip side of that is that we continue to expect things immediately. Whilst we have created a niche for ourselves through the latest technology, we think we can have the same in our relationships.

We can never have instant gratification in our relationships, instead we must work at those. Patience, empathy and understanding in relationships needs to be cultivated and nurtured.

Instead we should look at how we can be more patient; how we can be more kind; how we can be more understanding; and who and what matters to us most in our life. It's time we change the way we think.

OUR SELECTIVE DEEDS

Whether we think about it, or even realise it, we are selective about a lot of things. We're selective about what we eat, how we spend our time, how we spend our money. We're even selective about our deeds.

Perhaps we should consciously start to ask ourselves why we're selective about those things. Selective deeds must be purpose-based, we should strive to prioritise good deeds.

We should be here to help others so that when we're no longer around, we've made a difference. Good deeds show we have empathy and compassion: that we have integrity and that we want to be good people.

We will always make a positive impact when we do good deeds. The saying that 'it's better to give than to receive' is right. Researchers in the United States now say that giving to charity, or spending money on others, makes us feel better, more than if we were to buy things for ourselves. Therefore, helping others is beneficial for our own mental and physical health. (Source: https://positivepsychologyprogram.com)

When we help others, we are promoting physiological changes in the brain that are associated with happiness. Long term, these feelings are followed by longer periods of calm that lead to better health and wellbeing.

Helping others distracts us from our own problems, encourages us to lead a more active life, and improves self-esteem and confidence, which in turn improves competence. It also allows us to engage in meaningful activities and helps us improve social support to our community.

A good deed has a positive impact on our perceptions, which gives us a more positive outlook on life. Helping those who are less fortunate makes us realise how lucky we are and stops us from focusing on ourselves.

Good deeds promote positive emotions and help us reduce stress. Reducing stress boosts immunity, protecting us from disease.

MENTALITY EFFECTS CHANGE

Too often, we operate on the assumption that someone else is the cause of a problem, and fail to think about our own behaviour, or consider that our mentality can effect change. If we consistently fall into this trap, we will fail to effect any positive change. It's wrong to shine the torch on others when the problem may often lie with us.

It is our mindset, made up of thoughts, beliefs and expectations, which is the lens through which we see and think about things. Our life experiences affect how we will live and the decisions we will make every day.

According to cognitive neuroscientists, we are conscious of only about 5 per cent of cognitive activity, so most of our decisions, actions, emotions, and behaviour depends on the 95 per cent of brain activity that goes beyond our conscious thinking. (Source: http://www.simplifyinginterfaces.com)

Our experiences and childhood conditioning are the reasons we follow the same unconscious patterns and behaviours, and why we fail to make any positive changes.

When we live our lives without consciously giving thought to our behaviour, our mindset, based on our previous experiences, will remain stagnant. It is because we hear and repeat the same negative stories from our past over and over, that the same negative narratives are reinforced, but it won't be the case for all.

Whilst that happens, we can never effect positive mental change.

DEALING WITH CRITICAL PEOPLE

When someone is being overly critical, it is often because we don't stop them and because they know they can get away with it, unless we learn to object. In those circumstances, we must either understand the underlying message, ignore the message, or as a last resort, disengage.

Critical people don't think about what they're going to say before they say it. They'll bleat something out, then think about what they've said after they've said it, by which time it's too late to change anything.

But being critical of others stems from how we feel about ourselves. It's also a reflection of what we're dealing with at the time. If we're having a hard time working through our issues, we're going to feel angry. We take our anger out on those we love.

There is often a bigger picture to someone's anger and emotions. We don't just let off steam because we want to hurt someone. We won't always know why we're letting off steam, but letting off steam comes from our subconscious thinking: if our childhood experiences, or recent experiences, are negative, it is those experiences that will make us angry.

Unfortunately, when we're angry, all it takes is a split second to lash out, but it can take a lifetime to make amends. We must all take responsibility for our behaviour.

HOLDING A GRUDGE

My mum used to quote the saying 'no one goes to school to be a parent', but that puts children at a disadvantage. It tells children that however their parents parent, they're supposed to be OK with it. But it's not always OK, because children's lives are shaped by how they are parented.

In the context of spirituality, we all have free will to change how we do things: so do parents. Because children aren't always in a position to talk to their parents about how they're parented, it is important that parents parent well, and do the best they can.

Where children may hold grudges against their parents, it's crucial they understand that grudges turn into anger and anger into bitterness. These are conversations that parents should prioritise having with their children. Parents should always be approachable.

LIVING WITH NO REGRETS

For many years, I lived with guilty feelings and constant regrets that left me agitated, stressed and angry. Each day felt like a new battle. Every way I turned, my disappointments and failings continued to stare back at me.

I couldn't get rid of the guilt, particularly surrounding my schooling. It was constantly clouding my judgment on new situations, but thankfully the more spiritual I became, the more things slowly began to change for me.

I began to understand that my years of guilt had everything to do with my lack of control as a child and the decisions that were being made. Throughout my childhood, I had never made a decision for myself or been given a choice as to which path I went down. I was never encouraged to think for myself.

Unfortunately, any guilt or regrets we carry, regardless of whose guilt it is, will keep us stuck in the past. Although it took me many years to let go of the guilt, when I did, it finally felt like a release.

As my perceptions began to change, so too did my life. Slowly, I found the courage to begin to change some of the things that were holding me back.

Now I see the decisions I make as stepping stones to yet more change and more positive lessons for me to learn. As I evolve and grow spiritually, I also rely on my intuition to help me pave the way so that I live with no regrets moving forward.

REMOVING THE BLINDFOLD

Is it because we become so attached to our limited ideologies that we can fail to look at the whole? When we come to accept an ideology as the sole truth, when other people's facts contradict our beliefs no matter how plausible their ideologies are, we will fail to remove the blindfold.

Even when their facts contradict our current beliefs and we feel threatened, we're still not prepared to remove the blindfold. But just imagine how big the world becomes when we're willing to shift our ideology past our own personal beliefs.

It is a big world out there, it's important we learn about it. Removing the blindfold allows us to engage unconditionally in what's beyond our four walls and allows for emotional and spiritual growth.

We're telling the world we're open to possibilities beyond what we think we know and that says a lot about us. Whilst the blindfold is on, we're not choosing to look inwards at our thought process and that has the potential to set events of a negative cycle in motion.

Through a blindfold that's permanently fixed, we condition ourselves to self-limiting beliefs, without looking for further explanation. When we take the blindfold off, and we're looking at our lives in the whole, we're able to see its flaws, rather than just accept our self-limiting beliefs.

Self-limiting beliefs are false ideologies. I am sure we all have someone in our midst whose opinions are based on self-limiting ideologies, who are not willing to think about or consider other people's views.

So, if the ideology you follow has been there for far too long and your life isn't taking shape, or isn't how you want it to be, remember to take the blindfold off.

'This is my simple religion. There is no need for temples; no need for complicated philosophy. Our own brain, our own heart is our temple; the philosophy is kindness.'

THE DALAI LAMA

OWN YOUR APOLOGIES

It is never right for us to throw our wrongdoings at someone else and expect them to apologise for us. Instead we must apologise for our own words and actions.

Our apologies must be honest and truthful. We've got to mean the apology. An apology that is anything but honest and truthful isn't worth making. A true apology is universal and recognisable. It changes the way we think about ourselves and the way other people feel about us.

An apology that's true doesn't include the word 'but'. 'But' cancels out the apology and introduces an excuse. A true apology keeps the focus on our words and actions and not on the other person's response. It is important we learn to own our behaviour and response.

A true apology isn't about apportioning blame. It is about us recognising our part in the action and apologising for what we've done.

There is no point in apologising if we choose to repeat the same behavioural patterns. An apology should be supported by corrective action, so others are aware that change will follow. Apologies shouldn't be used to silence another person.

Because an apology is part of the healing process, no matter who is doing the apologising, it is important we understand the words behind the apology and know why the apology is there.

HAVING THE LAST WORD

How many of us know someone who, no matter what, needs to have the last word? Having the last word is a habit: it's an environmental and cultural problem that comes from stubbornness or background. When it comes to family, we probably already know who must have the last word.

However, when we give the other person the last word, we stop the conversation in its tracks. It also takes the heat out of what could turn into a battleground. For those who need to have the last word, it's usually because they have an opinion on everything.

When we decide not to have the last word, we take away the stress associated with needing to have it. It will never put those who insist on having the last word in a good light. There is no intrinsic value to it. Having the last word is about someone's exaggerated self-importance.

HOW STRESS AFFECTS OUR DNA

It has long been documented that stress weakens the immune system and can make us ill. Now researchers think it has a major impact on our DNA.

A study by Duke University Medical Centre in North Carolina, dated 22 August 2011, conclude that stress stimulates the secretion of adrenaline, which if not controlled can interfere with our DNA. (Source: https://www.dukehealth.org)

Stress is not tangible, we cannot see it and nine times out of ten we don't even know we're stressed. Others might think that if we don't talk about it, then we can't be stressed, but a bad word, even stubbornness, can be stress; we just don't always know that is what we're experiencing.

So how does stress affect us? Well, it affects everyone differently. We know that stress can cause heart disease, but generally many of us don't understand how stress and stressful situations cause physical and emotional problems.

The following may be of interest:

→ Around 43 per cent of adults suffer with the adverse health effects brought about by stress;

→ Stress can be linked to accidents, lung ailments, heart disease, cirrhosis of the liver, mental illness and suicide;

→ Between 75 and 90 per cent of doctors' visits are due to stress related illness.

To some extent stress is a necessary evil, although too much of it can and does play havoc with our health. In society, stress isn't easy to avoid, but it is important we understand how to deal with it.

Our inability to handle stress is detrimental to our health in the longer term.

INDECISIVE TENDENCIES

I am sure we've all been indecisive at some point. I know one or two people who struggle with making decisions, but not being able to make any decision at all can impact our lives.

It's all to do with self-confidence. We must have faith in ourselves and our abilities. Faith to trust our own thought process, rather than be led by other people: faith to believe that the decisions we make are right for us.

There is no wrong decision, because as soon as we decide, it becomes the right decision. We need to stop doubting ourselves, we need to bring about more self-confidence. We must learn to follow our gut instinct, then any decisions we make we will follow through.

Also, it is important we ignore other people's thoughts on our decisions, unless we know we have their support. Depending on another person's motive, it's easy for others to put us off making our own decisions.

Just because we make a decision that doesn't accord with another person's, doesn't mean our decision is wrong. It could be that our decision is wrong for someone else, but it's the right one for us.

Whatever happens, it's our life for us to make our own decisions. For those of us who are indecisive, we must try to at least stop being indecisive and instead make and stand by our own decisions.

BEING ACCEPTED

I was a pleasing child, always looking for acceptance because I was insecure. I was insecure because I was navigating a childhood with a disability I didn't know I had.

However we need to be accepted, it's something we crave for at different times. When things are good and we're making headway, we seem to want and need less acceptance.

Being accepted can make us feel safe and protected, but it isn't something we can always rely on. We must rely on ourselves and our own thinking for us to find and have acceptance. I believe how we are brought up is very much the catalyst for our acceptance. Where people recognise and understand their experiences they will be more accepting.

Although what happens in our past is the reason people struggle with acceptance, we must try to be more open-minded about our experiences. Referring to the past, when we come to understand why something happened the way it did, we will find a way to bring about acceptance. Although it is often difficult to achieve acceptance, so that we can move forward, we must strive to achieve it.

Acceptance is something we acquire if we fit the mould, rather than something given in abundance. But the opposite of acceptance is rejection and that can be bad for our mental health, if we're not sure how to deal with it.

We must also look at being accepted in its wider context. To avoid feeling isolated, excluded and lonely, we must come to understand the universe and how our lives fit into that.

Because acceptance is not inclusive, we must learn to like and accept ourselves. Society needs to be inclusive, so that acceptance is par for the course and open to everyone.

VALUING SANITY ABOVE GREED

I have always valued sanity above greed. As a child, I was unconsciously already laying down the foundations of a more spiritual life, but I didn't consciously understand that's what it was.

In the early years, family is the most important influence, until we begin to spread our wings. But as we grow up, it is important we continue to stick to our moral standing and values. It's easy for our allegiance to people and things to replace those. Instead of a need to want more things, remember to think about and work on yourself.

As we unconsciously begin to acquire more things, we will continue to ignore our emotions and our sanity. As we go through life we may draw more importance to things than people, or even ourselves, although there are exceptions.

Sadly, when we put greed above sanity and think less about the importance of value, we're not happy to live the simple life, we want more.

MY SPIRITUAL BELIEFS

Given my life experiences, I have a right to be upset. However, instead of dwelling on the negativity, I have chosen a more spiritual path for myself.

My spiritual beliefs have helped me find understanding, where before I couldn't see or understand. Spirituality is a road of self-discovery, recognising the deepest of values in the human spirit as opposed to material or physical things, so that we aspire to life in its simplest form, without complications or negativity.

Spirituality is about giving without needing to receive, and about having inner peace. I draw inspiration from the smallest of things and look for the lessons I am shown, even if those lessons don't always make sense to me. My beliefs continue to help me focus away from my physical form, and that helps take away any stress.

I have days where my beliefs are put to the test because of my experiences and because I deal with cerebral palsy and autism, but I am drawn back like a magnet. I don't always understand everything I deal with, but my spiritual beliefs help me understand my experiences more, so that my life can run more smoothly.

'Those who contemplate the beauty of the earth find reserves of strength that will endure as long as life lasts. There is something infinitely healing in the repeated refrains of nature – the assurance that dawn comes after night, and spring after winter.'

RACHEL CARSON

MORALITY AND SPIRITUALITY

Living a moral life is synonymous with spirituality. So, in a broad sense, when I talk about morality, I am defining spirituality. Spirituality has everything to do with morality.

Morality is everything that spirituality is. Being moral allows us to live honestly and purely in a world that doesn't always take notice. Keeping morality close to us, in the hub of everyday life, serves to remind us that morality and spirituality can pave the way for us to be happy, content and at peace.

Being moral and spiritual helps us to stay grounded in a world that is less than perfect, morally and spiritually. It is something we should all practice. Morality and spirituality, if continually practiced, will make us better people.

CHOOSING TO BE MORAL

As long as we know right from wrong and have a conscience, we will follow a moral compass. Without basic rules surrounding morality, there will always be chaos in our homes and in our lives.

We're not all instinctively moral, but we can choose to be moral. It is all a question of how we choose to relate and behave towards other people and in society. We must want to care about others and ourselves. We must want to have empathy, compassion and tolerance. We must want to follow and incorporate moral tolerance.

We need to strive to understand how our conscience plays its part in our moral compass. If the conscience alerts us to something that it knows is wrong, we can and should choose to change our behaviour. It is our conscience that challenges us to change how we see other people and how moral we will choose to be.

JUDGMENT AND SPIRITUALITY

As someone who is spiritual, I have never tried to make anyone believe what I believe, or judge someone for what they believe. It's simply not my way.

As individuals, we will grow, we will evolve. Who we are today is not who we will be tomorrow, or who we were yesterday. Every soul has a spirit. It's important we start on a path to spiritual awareness, knowledge and insight.

Spirituality paves the way for understanding how life works, what our lessons, are and how we will be with each other. For those who judge others, they do so because they are less aware of their spiritual path and values. Judging someone else is never the right or best path for your spiritual journey.

We will spend a lifetime forming judgments and beliefs. Our beliefs are an interpretation of our experiences and therefore may never be right for anyone else. Judgments are based on beliefs and beliefs are based on individual perceptions.

It is not for us to try to convert anyone else to believe what we believe, or for anyone else to convert or judge us back.

SPIRITUALITY AND ME

I never tire of writing about or wanting to learn more about spirituality, particularly because spirituality has brought a certain calm to my life.

Spirituality has given me the power to choose how I see and create my own realities. It has shown me that my life reflects what I put out into the world. When others think the same way, it's like meeting someone for the first time and realising how much we have in common.

When you begin to take an interest and understand the bigger picture, how that ties you to the universe and each other, and where your lives fit in, you may want to know how it all works, asking questions such as, 'What is my purpose?' and 'Where did we come from?'

When you can begin to show such qualities as love, tolerance, forgiveness, patience and understanding for others, you know you've become aware of the spiritual concept and all that being spiritual is about.

Anyone can subscribe to it. Spirituality gives a whole new meaning of how we get to live our life and how we can get the best out of what we have.

SPIRITUALITY AND RELIGION

It is said by some that religion and spirituality are total opposites. Historically, we were spiritual long before we found religion.

Spirituality can be described as an attachment to one's inner soul through life and how we choose to live it. Spirituality allows us to look at a wealth of opportunities so that we can live life in its most simplest form, whereas religion is associated with the concerns of a life through faith, culture and society.

When you can accept yourself physically, emotionally and spiritually, you know you're on the spiritual path. The spiritual path allows us to accept the things we cannot change, deal with the things we can, and give of ourselves without needing anything in return.

Spirituality isn't something that just happens, it's a journey of different experiences, culminating in emotional tranquillity and peace that comes from within, allowing us to choose how we see the world and other people. It sets us apart from others, through our attitude and how we conduct ourselves.

Spirituality helps us understand ourselves, our lives and others whilst we follow its path, and that puts us in tune with ourselves and our surroundings.

CATS AND SPIRITUALITY

Cats can teach us so much about life.

When my mum was terminally ill, Pumpkin came into our lives. She had already been named by the rescue centre, although my children called her Homey. For us, owning a cat was a life-changing decision and we've never looked back.

She was a rescue cat that picked us out when we went to the cattery. She instantly attached herself to my daughter. She looked neglected, had a skin condition, and had been found wandering the streets.

She came into our lives and changed us forever. Just by watching her I have become even more spiritually aware. We have all learned so much from her simple needs of love, warmth, food and shelter.

Cats are known for being spiritual. I love to observe my cat to see how she interacts with her world. They have a uniquely powerful aura which takes away negativity and they carry a big energy field. Cats can help us see our world differently, their needs are simple and uncomplicated. They can teach us the values of living a simple and stress-free life, as long as we're receptive and open to their aura and energy.

These values lend themselves to a more spiritual, harmonious and peaceful life. Spirituality isn't a religion. It relates to or affects the human spirit or soul, as opposed to physical or material things.

Spirituality is a path towards self-actualisation, allowing those who practice to continue to focus on their internal values and so that they become better people.

Dedicated to my cat Pumpkin, known as *'Homey'*.

> 'We are not human beings having a spiritual experience. We are spiritual beings having a human experience.'
>
> PIERRE TEILHARD de CHARDIN

BEAUTY FROM WITHIN

There is no point in us looking beautiful if every time we open our mouths something ugly comes out.

My mind goes to a film called *The Elephant Man*. Marred by tumours that left him permanently disfigured, Joseph Carey Merrick was frightening to look at. He was a gentle soul, yet society treated him like a freak. Despite this, his wonderful personality shone through.

The film is based on a real story and it teaches us about life, compassion, humility and humanity, and above all one man's determination to prove that just because he looked different on the outside, it didn't mean that he was not worthy of love, admiration and friendship. He was a kind, caring and a good-natured man, who was simply looking for acceptance.

He wanted to live a normal life without being under the glare of the media spotlight. He wanted people to accept him. He wanted to live his life without being rebuked, stared at, ridiculed or provoked by those who thought he should be in a circus just so that people could stare and laugh at him.

The beauty inside is what counts and we don't place enough emphasis on it. We're too quick to judge people on appearance. But we can all have beautiful qualities. Pressure from society to behave in a certain way is not an excuse, but we may behave as if it is.

We must begin to understand what life is about; we must also take the time to learn about ourselves and how we can go about making changes from the inside out, because everything starts from there.

LOOK FOR THE BEAUTY

We will never achieve inner beauty if we fail to see the beauty in other things. It's very easy when we're busy not to see the world in all its perfection.

We spend too much time living in our heads and not enough time soaking in the atmosphere of nature and the world around us: and in doing so we will fail to look at and connect with the little things; the things that contribute positively to our lives and allow us to see the bigger picture.

We should resonate with our consciousness and take the time to look for and see the beauty in our surroundings. When we choose to look insightfully and carefully at an object, a landscape, a structure, there will always be beauty we can appreciate.

Although I have difficulty walking long distances, I do like to take notice of the things around me when I am out on a walk.

WHY DON'T WE ALWAYS SEE THE BEAUTY?

When we form expectations, or live with preconceived ideas, we've already restricted our thoughts on the world around us. We've already reduced what we see to very little.

There is so much to see, and yet we ignore the things that can make us more settled and complete. The next time you're outside, think about and look at what's around you, connect with your world. If you're going out for a walk notice the flowers, the colours, the contours, the smells and the sounds.

I love to walk around the lake at my local park and take in the scenery; look at the ducks, notice their beaks, the reflection of the sunlight on the water and the shape of the leaves on the trees, and the sounds of nature.

If you're near some woods take a look at the trees, look at the intricate detail of how the leaves are formed, and their different colours: things you wouldn't necessarily think to look at. The more we practise and make this part of our daily routine, the more we'll notice things without us having to think.

And by seeing what is beautiful we will have a sense of appreciation, peace and gratitude, not to mention empathy, compassion and tolerance. Those are the things we miss out on if we don't tap into our consciousness.

It's all about becoming aware, embracing the simple things, noticing and seeing the beauty in those things. It is important we look for the beauty in everything that touches our lives.

BEING BEAUTIFUL INSIDE AND OUT

Being beautiful isn't just about having a beautiful face or a beautiful body. Beauty comes from the mind; beauty is etched on our souls, and reveals itself in our actions toward others. Be beautiful.

Below are some ways you can work on being beautiful from the inside out:

→ Be grateful for what you have, rather than what you'd like to have;

→ Learn to accept what you have and your life in its entirety;

→ Keep your thoughts grounded;

→ Accept your lessons, they are there to help you grow;

→ Find time to sit and concentrate on yourself so that you can regroup your thoughts;

→ Learn to see the good in everyone;

→ Practice compassion, empathy, tolerance and patience;

→ Learn to meditate;

→ Don't judge, pass an opinion, or be critical of others just because you're hurting;

→ Learn to accept your flaws;

→ Stop being angry, bitter or malicious towards someone else.

Being beautiful inside and out and being happy with ourselves will allow us to focus on others more positively. Learn to put yourself in someone else's shoes and then ask yourself if the way you're treating others is the way you would want others to treat you.

KARMA

According to the teachings of Buddhism, karma is part environmental, part nature and nurture, and part hereditary.

It is the result of how we conduct ourselves and of our own past actions.

Generally, we will do things without thinking about what we're doing, but as far as Buddhism is concerned, nothing happens to a person that he doesn't deserve. Karma knows us and will always work on the motives behind the deed.

But often, we will make decisions and fail to think about the consequences.

The cause of the visible effect may also not be confined to the present time. It may be traced to a proximate, or 'remote past birth'; in other words, something that happened to us in a past life.

But to understand karma we must ask ourselves these questions:

→ What is the cause of the inequality that exists in the world?

→ Why might one person be brought up in the lap of luxury and another in complete poverty?

→ Why is someone born disabled?

→ Why should one person be born with saintly tendencies and another with criminal?

The world is shrouded in inequality. Inequality is either purely accidental or has a cause. That said, no sensible person would consciously attribute such unevenness or inequality by accident or through blind chance.

In other words, we are part of the problem and we are part of the solution. We create our own heaven and hell. We are instrumental in our own lives. We are the architects of our own fate. We must act with compassion and tolerance. We must come together.

We must also be the change we want to see in the world. We must want to do and be better. We must all work together so we can make the world safer.

It's not just for us, either. It is important and we must want to leave the world a better place for future generations to come.

THE TEACHING OF KARMA

As a child, I was always aware of the existence of something bigger. Although I couldn't quite put my finger on it, or what I now know to be Buddhism, I was already living by some of its teachings and beliefs. Now I use it in everyday life. It helps me understand and come to terms with most if not all of my experiences.

Karma, part of the teachings of Buddhism, is a belief system that for every action there is a reaction. It is a belief that if we put out kindness, kindness will find us. If we tell lies, it won't be long before someone lies about us. Karma bounces back when we least expect. It may not happen when we want it to, but it's something we can't avoid or stop.

If we attach our life to unsavoury people, when their karma bounces back to teach them their lessons, so will ours by association. It's part of how the universe works. We also live karma in everyday life.

I believe that when we use compassion, forgiveness and kindness, we set a more positive precedent to bring good back into our lives. Karma is powerful, and not something we should work against. If we all took on board the teachings of karma, we would continue to contribute to our lives very differently.

Karma allows us to take responsibility for the way we choose to live our lives. If you believe you live your own karma, you will choose and want to live a more spiritual life and make better choices for you and your family.

When we continue to blame others and fail to take responsibility for ourselves, we will continue to mentally and emotionally struggle. When we blame karma for our difficulties and struggles, without taking control back for ourselves, karma will be responsible for more pain and physical hardships.

WORKING ON THE SOUL

I believe that we are born with a loving, caring and happy soul, but our experiences in life affects our soul. Those experiences will begin to reflect and make up our personalities.

It is through those experiences that bad patterns can be formed. The trouble is that we're often too busy trying to work on our own survival that we don't look beyond our opinions and attitudes, to what truly lies within us. But we are all capable of changing how we perceive ourselves and other people, regardless of those patterns.

Our attitudes, opinions and approaches form what people see on the outside and that is what we show family, friends and the world. What we should be doing is working from the outside in, so that what people see on the inside is what they see on the outside.

I was an angry child, living with a disability I didn't know I had, but inside there was a soft side, different from my siblings, which others rarely saw. Every now and again that soft side would come out: I'd be sweet and caring and my family would get to see that side of me. Just before my father passed those were his very words.

But it has taken a long time for me to unwrap the sweet, caring side. I know I was quite a challenging child, but no one took the time to understand why. I am disappointed, but after years of reflection, working on myself and through each individual experience, I have been able to put a lot of this behind me.

SPIRITUAL AWARENESS

Spiritual growth is a process of inner awakening, where we start to become aware of our 'inner-self'. Being aware of our inner-self allows us to develop a higher awareness so that we're able to tap into our unconscious thinking: it enables us to go beyond what's in our conscious thoughts, helping to bring an understanding of who we really are and what makes us, us.

We all have the ability, but usually that part of who we really are is tucked away behind the ego-personality. Being spiritual allows us to listen to our inner thoughts, so that we're constantly tuned in to them.

Having spiritual beliefs helps us to become better, more compassionate people, and live a more peaceful and tranquil life. Being spiritually aware helps take away our fear, anxiety and stress. It also helps us to compose ourselves, so that we are able to remain calm under pressure, with whatever we have to deal with.

NATURALLY INTUITIVE

Intuition is something we all have, but not something we're always aware of. It can be used to help us successfully navigate our lives.

Have you ever had that feeling when you know that something is right for you, even though you're not sure why, or you instinctively get the feeling you must go down a certain path? It is our intuition that lets us know this. It allows us to make changes, even though we may be hesitant and want to resist change at first.

Intuition is defined as 'a thing that one knows or considers likely from instinctive feeling rather than conscious reasoning.' (Source: https://thriveglobal.com) It steers us on the path we are meant to take without us questioning why.

Intuition isn't something we need to use every day or tap into continually, but we must want to listen to it, learn and be open to it.

When we ignore its presence, it usually means we're not in tune or prepared to listen. It could be because we are constantly resistant to change and, instead, we repeat old habits and ignore instinctive feelings.

Instinctive feelings can bring about new events that we didn't see, together with new opportunities. To let light and peace in, we must learn to follow our instinctive feelings.

For those who meditate, or who practise by listening, their intuition should grow stronger. Life is more rewarding when we listen to our intuition.

Intuition paves the way for us to have an easier life; it allows for spiritual growth and the more we use our intuition, the more peace we will have.

SPIRITUAL CONNECTIONS

Soulful connections make us kinder, more compassionate and wiser: they help us change the way we function individually, and how we see ourselves, our partners and our lives.

A spiritual connection is when two souls are attracted and are in sync with each other. Two people with a spiritual connection are not just aligned; they bond emotionally and spiritually through soulful connections. Those relationships are the most enduring.

Unless two people practice and work towards the same spiritual values, it will be difficult for their souls to connect in this way, but it is perfectly achievable.

The word 'spiritual' for some people may sound scary, but in fact it's the total opposite. A lack of understanding can make it scary. A spiritual partner is an ally for personal growth, when both partners decide they want to work together, to be the best that they can be.

Those relationships are the most enduring and are our most soulful connections.

'The moment you doubt whether you can fly, you cease forever to be able to do it.'

J M BARRIE

MY VALUES

Everything I write in 'The CP Diary' pays homage to my experiences and emotional wellbeing. On the back of my experiences, each blog carries a value and message.

I love to write about the things that mean something to me, like the values placed upon us as individuals and how those values play out in our lives: the old-fashioned values of caring and making a difference matter to me.

When I was a little girl, I lived in a modest house. My parents weren't rich and as far as I knew, they weren't poor either, but I had it instilled in me that to buy something, I had to earn it first. I never asked for anything, but that wasn't bad, because it taught me not to value materialistic things. I had to find my happiness elsewhere.

I never really understood what my parents' values were. I'm not sure you do as a child. It's not something we talked about. But I knew family was important to my mum.

I took my own values very seriously, but also dealing with a disability I didn't know I had meant I saw the world from a completely different angle. From an early age, because I knew I was different, I began to hone in on the value of relationships. I tried to reach out to others, to talk about my disability, but after a while when that didn't happen, it became obvious that I needed to become my own emotional support.

As a child, it wasn't obvious to me why I always aimed to please, conform and look for acceptance more than my other siblings. I assumed it had something to do with me being different. Now, looking back, I am confident that's what it was.

Today, looking after and making sure my own family are happy are what I value the most.

MY RULES OF THE ROAD

Being spiritual, my values have always been important to me, so I thought I'd note down the values that help me bring and maintain peace in my life:

→ Whenever you help someone, do it with good grace;

→ When you apologise to someone, mean it;

→ Being aware of our lessons;

→ Not dwelling, but learning from failure;

→ Never belittle another person's thoughts or beliefs;

→ When talking to someone, always make sure you listen;

→ Be attentive and show you care through compassion;

→ Get to know someone first before you pass judgment. Better still, don't pass judgment;

→ If someone isn't willing to meet you halfway, their friendship isn't for keeps;

→ Always be yourself;

→ Think about yourself from time to time;

→ Think about those who need emotional support and be willing to offer it if you can;

→ Be a shoulder to cry on, you never know when you might need one back;

→ Don't judge others by your own standards. It is important for others to have a fair trial;

→ Don't pull other people into your misery, or pull them down because you're feeling bad;

→ Work on seeing only the positive, and if the positive turns out to be less than positive, always look for the silver lining;

→ Speak your own truth;

→ Don't compromise on your own values or morals just to please others;

→ Never leave something said in anger. Going back to make amends is always the best policy.

THE GOLDEN RULE

My mum used to constantly quote the 'Golden Rule', saying, 'Do unto others as you would have them do unto you.' I believe she was right; the 'Golden Rule' should be applied to all aspects of our lives.

For example, helping an elderly neighbour, a family member, or a colleague at work. Following the 'Golden Rule' allows us to be kind and concerned for others, it helps us grow emotionally: it gives us a feeling of satisfaction that we're helping others and generally making a difference.

It shows others that we're prepared to put them first if they need us to. If applied on an everyday basis, the 'Golden Rule' will empower us to become better people. On a more global footing it will make our communities better places to live. It will always have a ripple effect on everything we do. It will also empower us to make better choices.

Using the 'Golden Rule' will give us more confidence to believe in ourselves and to find inner peace. It's a lifestyle choice that will not only bring harmony into our lives, but into the lives of everyone we touch.

FEAR OF FAILING

How many of us quit before we have a chance to fail, because we feel we're doomed for failure in the first place? We're not always aware in the beginning of how to succeed. We give up too easily.

But failing is a catalyst of the learning process. It's not to say that we have to fail every time if we are to become successful, but failing enables us to understand that life isn't all about success and that if we want to be successful, we have to learn how to fail first.

Circumstances are forever changing. Nothing inherently stays the same and with circumstances that change, we must change, too. Generally, we stay within our comfort zones and work to keep ourselves there, but we must also think about coming out. Success comes from being able to leave our comfort zones: and playing it safe for too long means we will stagnate.

Change is a fact of life, not always easy to accept because of fear and apprehension, but how we work and address change can determine whether we will be successful or not. To tackle any form of change, we must leave our comfort zones.

How many times have you promised yourselves you'll do something, but never follow through? It is often not because we're lazy, but because we're too afraid, particularly if what we're doing is something we've never done before. We must learn to experience life with its ups and downs, because that's how we will grow and if that means leaving our comfort zones every now and again, then that's what we must do.

Our greatest challenge is the fear we feel, but we can overcome it and be successful. It is often the fear we feel that holds us back and stops us achieving success.

'When I was five years old, my mother always told me that happiness was the key to life. When I went to school, they asked me what I wanted to be when I grew up. I wrote down "happy". They told me I didn't understand the assignment, and I told them they didn't understand life.'

JOHN LENNON

A PASSION FOR LIFE

Passion allows us to feel courage and follow our convictions, and gives us a strong sense of self so that we can take those first steps out into the world.

Passion comes from feeling confident, from knowing everything we need to know about ourselves, understanding our experiences and our lives. For some of us, our passions are there, we innately know what we want to do, but for others they must work on understanding what their passions are.

Passion also comes from working on our strengths, weaknesses and values. Passion is what makes us feel good about ourselves. When we have passion, the things that we do will come naturally and effortlessly. Passion empowers, it motivates us.

When we are empowered, our personal strengths and passion are evident for everyone to see. If others are to believe in us, we must believe in ourselves first. When we have passion, our values become evident to those around us in the good deeds we do, in the way we handle ourselves.

EXPECTATIONS

How many of us know from an early age what we want to do when we grow up? With parental encouragement, children think and dream about their own futures. I remember being asked that same question by friends of the family as a child, and my father answering before I had a chance to speak.

We must all be encouraged to dream, to know what our potential is and to be encouraged to achieve it. Not only does potential encourage wider thought, but it also encourages us to be confident, independent and be more in control of our lives.

By the time I had reached my thirties, I hadn't achieved anything. It was when my mother became terminally ill and she told me mine 'was a difficult birth' that I intuitively understood, she was 'opening the door' for me to find out about my disability.

Without encouragement, if we have low expectations of ourselves, it is not so easy for us to pick ourselves back up. Some children will go through their childhood and believe what they're told and won't stop to question. Others will think about what they're being told and may question everything. With low expectations, we almost have to talk ourselves into believing that we can achieve and aspire to our dreams and goals.

My first goal was to find out what I had been dealing with for all those years. My second goal was to go back into education, and, at the point of diagnosis, my third goal was to set up and run my own website. My fourth goal is to have this book published. All of which I am immensely grateful to have achieved.

I believe anyone can change their expectations, but first we must learn how to change: a different approach to managing and raising our expectations is needed. We also must make sure that our goals and dreams are not beyond our reach, but within it.

OUR ENTRANCE AND EXIT

Some of us will be affected by our early years more than others. Through our background, environment and experiences, some of us will emotionally struggle. Our earlier experiences can and do shape who we are and how we will go on to behave.

But that can be no excuse for bad behaviour. It's a parent's duty to show children moral practices regardless of their own background. It's important that whatever issues a parent has, they try to sort them out so that their family don't have to pick up the pieces long after they're gone.

I find it upsetting when I hear stories where that doesn't happen. Although parents might carry problems that other family members won't always know about, they need to be dealt with, long before they're gone and not left for their children to sort out.

I also believe that no matter what circumstances we are born into, or what our story is, our entrance and exit are the most important, because together they shape who we are and how others will see and remember us. There is never an excuse for leaving behind an adverse impact. We only have to pick up a newspaper or listen to the media to know how some of those stories end.

Even though we may deal with neglect, abuse, or anxiety, we don't have to stay in that place. I have learned that whatever truths we uncover along the way, we must learn a more spiritual path, because that fundamentally helps shape our life and helps us with emotional and spiritual growth.

It is how we communicate with each other, how moral we are, and the good deeds we do for others, that sets the tone for our journey to enlightenment. And though our path may not run smooth and we might also have to deal with deceit, it is still possible for us to live a moral life.

'Emotional wealth is infinitely more gratifying and liberating than that of financial wealth.'

CLAUDIA STANKLER

UNDERSTANDING THE REASONS

When you learn to look into another person's soul and you learn more about them, it becomes easier to understand why they would choose to do something. But being able to forgive someone for something they've done may not apply in all cases, it depends on the deed.

I have come to understand that what happened to me wasn't personal. Although conscious decisions were taken for me not to know about my disability, I understand the reasoning. When we can understand the reasoning behind another person's deed, it makes how we feel that little bit easier.

I cannot remember what age I was when I had already reconciled that I might never learn about my disability. It's not something anyone should have to contemplate or work through. It is important we all reconcile our deeds, for the sake of others, and put right those deeds.

CHOOSE TO BE HAPPY

We should choose to be happy over being angry or sad. I didn't understand why as a child I was so angry. Fast forward to adulthood and I believe, see and understand things differently now.

How many of us react out of anger? We're quick to get our feelings out so that we may protect ourselves. We usually impart a reaction to something that's said, and that can be damaging. It is important that we are in control and understand how to deal with our emotions.

When we allow others to influence us, we are giving them power over our emotions, and that influences how we behave in return. When we take control of our emotions, we're less likely to emanate negative emotions.

We need to own our thoughts and deal with our feelings so that what others say doesn't affect our response. Our response is a habit that must be relearned.

LOOKING AT THE POSITIVES

Some of us will see the negatives before we see the positives, others will simply see life negatively and continue to see life negatively.

But it is often difficult for us to see or understand why our lives map out in a certain way, or the purpose of our experiences. Whatever happens, there is no point in looking back and wishing our lives were different, because that won't change anything, unless we look for the lessons.

For those who struggle to find the lessons or understand the reasons, they must look at what they have achieved through their accomplishments and continue to build their life around those.

WALK YOUR OWN PATH

As human beings we are unique. Even though we can experience similar things, we are still unique. No two people will see the same experiences in the same way. If we did, we'd all be clones of each other.

Unfortunately, expectations are put upon us from an early age to behave in a certain way, or follow a certain path. It is important we walk our own path, despite those external influences.

It is also important we put our own stamp on things, make our own mistakes and take responsibility for the decisions we make. Never be swayed into thinking your decision isn't right, just because someone else has offered you an opinion, or another choice, or doesn't agree with your decision.

Don't feel guilt-tripped into taking their path because you feel you may be letting them down. The only person you'll be letting down is yourself. If you don't put your own stamp on things, other people's core values will become yours.

If we're lucky enough to be born to parents who allow us to make our own decisions, we'll walk our own path in life as an adult. When we're not allowed to make our own decisions and we're expected to fall into line, it will always come at a cost.

If you have the opportunity, choose to be an independent thinker, so you can build your confidence and have faith in your own abilities. Take control of your thoughts, of your feelings and how you want to live your life, and you will.

'God grant me the serenity to accept the things I cannot change, the courage to change the things I can, and the wisdom to know the difference.'

REINHOLD NIEBUHR

AN UNDERSTANDING

If I had known about my cerebral palsy when it was initially diagnosed at the age of two, I would never have gone down the diagnosis route at the age of forty-six and I would never have started 'The CP Diary' and my personal cerebral palsy journey.

Although I wouldn't want others to have gone through my experiences, I do recognise the positives in having them. I also know that had my parents acted on my disability, and found out about all my symptoms, I would have had very little to think or write about. My thoughts and feelings, everything I have had to work through, have come about because I was never told of my diagnosis and then finding out the initial diagnosis was wrong. The correct diagnosis is 'mild hemiparesis cerebral palsy'. I could never have known this without the further research into my symptoms.

I know now that I also have autism. Although when I was born there was little known about autism, it is clear my case had nothing to do with that. Due to family circumstances I slipped through the net. Also, what happened to me, and the fact that I only got to find out about this as an adult, would be unlikely to happen again because children are now routinely diagnosed.

Although my parents have inadvertently paved the way for me to find out about my disability, there is no doubt that my journey down this path started the day I was born.

Decisions were made around my disability that didn't allow me to grow mentally, emotionally or spiritually, for me to be comfortable in my own skin. Fundamentally, human beings get things wrong, but I believe we have the power in us to find understanding. Mistakes are made and the human condition is inevitably flawed, but it's up to us as individuals to find ways to make things better. As my story shows, it can be done.

Working through my experiences has made for my deeper understanding and that allows for the jigsaw to be completed. I cannot change my experiences, what I went through, but I can continue to look for acceptance on the things I still struggle with. I'm not angry or bitter at what I've been through, that's not my way and there would be no point. Instead, I draw strength from my writing and use my experiences to bring understanding to why my life had to be this way.

Without my experiences to draw upon for inspiration, I couldn't have done and achieved what I have with my life, or with my blog. Trauma, or anything else you want to call it, is never OK: but I understand. I know that without my experiences, I would never have become an author, a writer and a blogger. And whilst I cannot change my experiences, my blogs act as a reminder that there is always a message, a silver lining, and a way through our experiences.

No child should have to live in the dark. Not knowing about my cerebral palsy or autism meant I needed to take the initiative, to learn about my diagnoses and to understand all of my symptoms. My symptoms needed to fit my experiences.

Over the years, although my brain had already compensated, I did have an inkling of how I presented. It was important to me that others understood 'me'. I wanted to know: I needed to understand myself.

I'm not sure how old I was when it began to dawn on me that I might never know about my disability and that I might have to go to the grave not knowing. I could never have foreseen then how my life was going to change, but I go back to hope. I also know that without writing this book, I could never have achieved this level of understanding.

I find it difficult to comprehend that while others knew my symptoms would not improve, I continued to believe that tomorrow was another day and that eventually I would get better. I always believed that what I had was temporary because I didn't know any different, and that gave me the hope. Then finding out at forty-six that I had cerebral palsy and knowing I would never get better, dashed the hopes I'd been living with as a child. Difficult to hear, and difficult to work through, I felt I had no choice but to pick myself back up.

Now, having overcome so many difficulties and having come through to tell 'a tale', I am proud of myself and my achievements, and the opportunities and the people I have come into contact with along the way. I am thankful.

ACKNOWLEDGEMENTS

To Brad, thanks for all the support and encouragement, for the endless hours of proofreading and the countless herbal teas.

To Dan and Claudia, watching you make successes of your own lives has been the inspiration and motivation behind my book.

I have my mum to thank, because without her words there would be no blog and no book. This is for you, Mum.

And to my cat, Pumpkin, for her spiritual inspiration.

ABOUT THE AUTHOR

 Ilana's cerebral palsy diagnosis was hidden from her until the age of forty-six. That diagnosis was a life-changing moment that allowed Ilana to look at her life experiences differently. Months after her diagnosis, she set up her website 'The CP Diary'. Ilana spends her days writing and blogging about things that contribute to her health and wellbeing. She uses her experiences to write, bringing clarity into her life. She writes about health and wellbeing, advocating positivity, empathy and understanding through her blog, and across social media. Ilana who is passionate about the environment and is an animal advocate, lives with her husband and their much-loved cat, in Yorkshire. When she is not writing, Ilana enjoys days out exploring the beautiful north Yorkshire countryside.

RESOURCES

United Cerebral Palsy

https://ucp.org/

Scope

https://www.scope.org.uk

Mind

https://www.mind.org.co.uk

Mencap

https://www.mencap.org.uk/

Find out more about RedDoor
Press and sign up to our
newsletter to hear about our
latest releases, author events,
exciting **competitions**
and more at

reddoorpress.co.uk

YOU CAN ALSO FOLLOW US:

 @RedDoorBooks

 Facebook.com/RedDoorPress

 @RedDoorBooks